# Michelangelo Pistoletto
## the Third Paradise

Marsilio

*The author would like to thank*
*Andrea Lupi and Ruggero Poi*
*for the precious collaboration*

*translation*
Huw Evans

*photo*
Claudio Abate
Enrico Amici
Marco Fedele di Catrano
Alessandro Lacirasella
Juan Esteban Sandoval

*cover*
Michelangelo Pistoletto drawing
the Third Paradise on a mirror,
photo Juan Esteban Sandoval


*First edition*: April 2010
isbn 978-88-317-0649

www.marsilioeditori.it

# Contents

# the Third Paradise

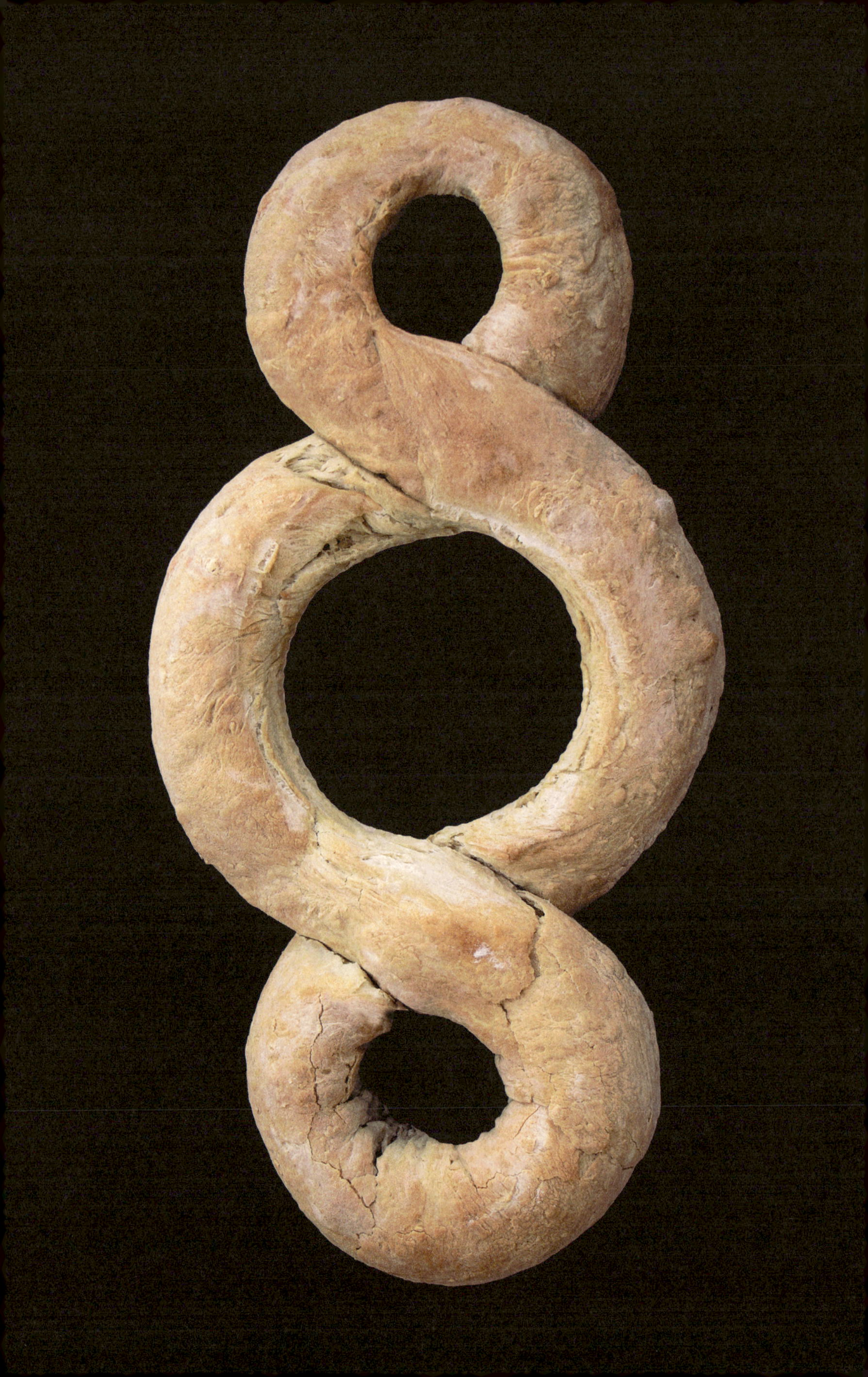

# Introduction

It is not the intention of this book to deal exhaustively with all the questions covered, but to serve as a guide that can help readers find their way at this critical juncture of an epoch-making transition which is growing increasingly dramatic. The words that they will read stem from the experience of a life that for decades now has been devoted to the responsible transformation of society through the generative function of art. With this book I aim to communicate the essential and decisive means of ushering in the Third Paradise, proposing new perspectives of thought and action that will induce in readers an awareness of their own role in the construction of a new age for humanity. In a situation of general disorientation and unsustainability that affects every area of communal life, the need is felt to identify values that can be shared. I hope to stimulate a debate on the themes of the environment, the survival of the human species on Earth, politics, economics, education and spirituality that will involve everyone who wishes to make a contribution to ensuring that the Third Paradise goes beyond its symbolic significance and becomes a reality.

# The Third Paradise is the new world

The symbol of the Third Paradise unites the human community

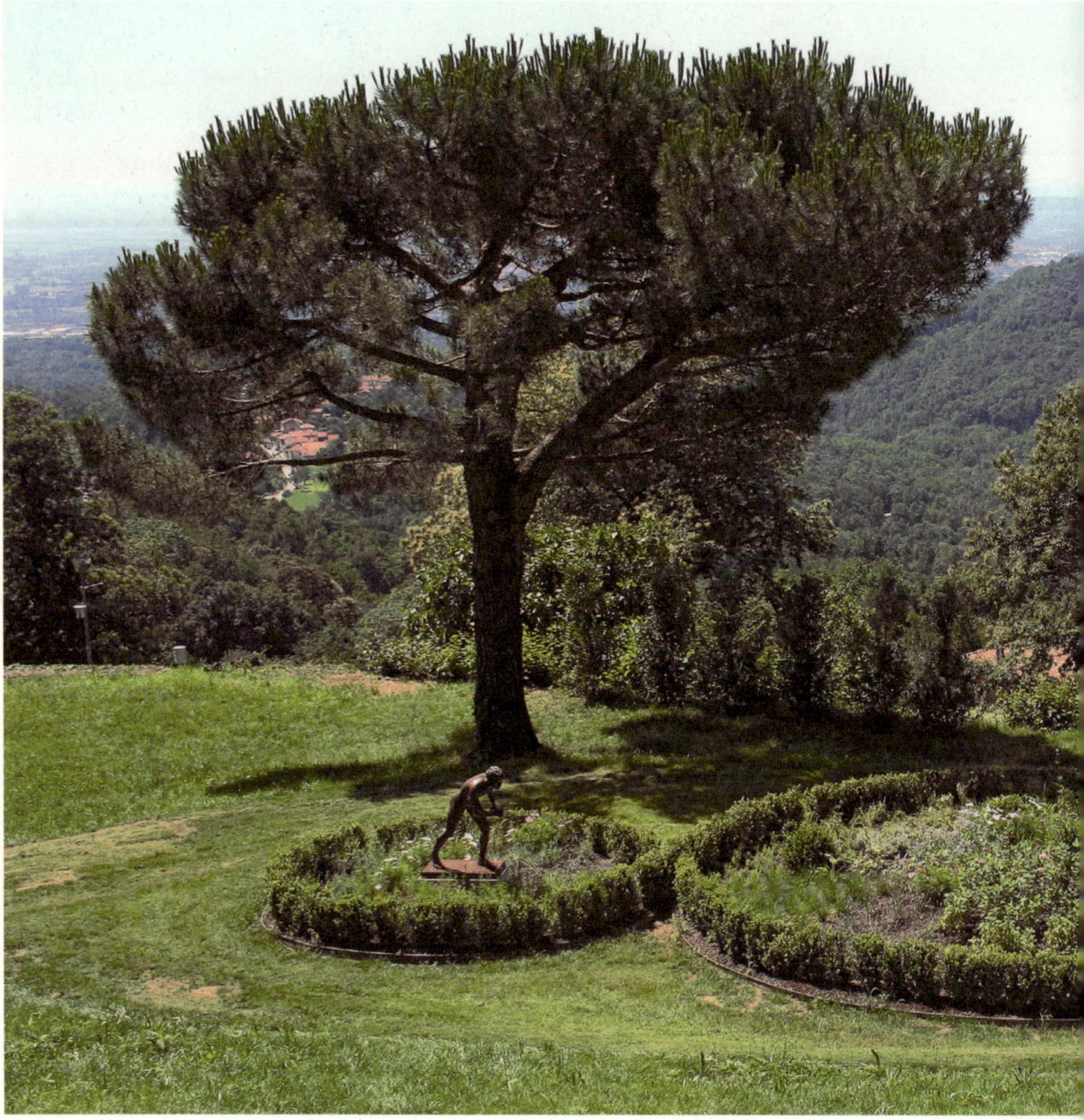

*Third Paradise Vegetable Plot*, Pettinengo (Biella), Villa Piazzo, associazione pacefuturo, 2008
photo: Alessandro Lacirasella

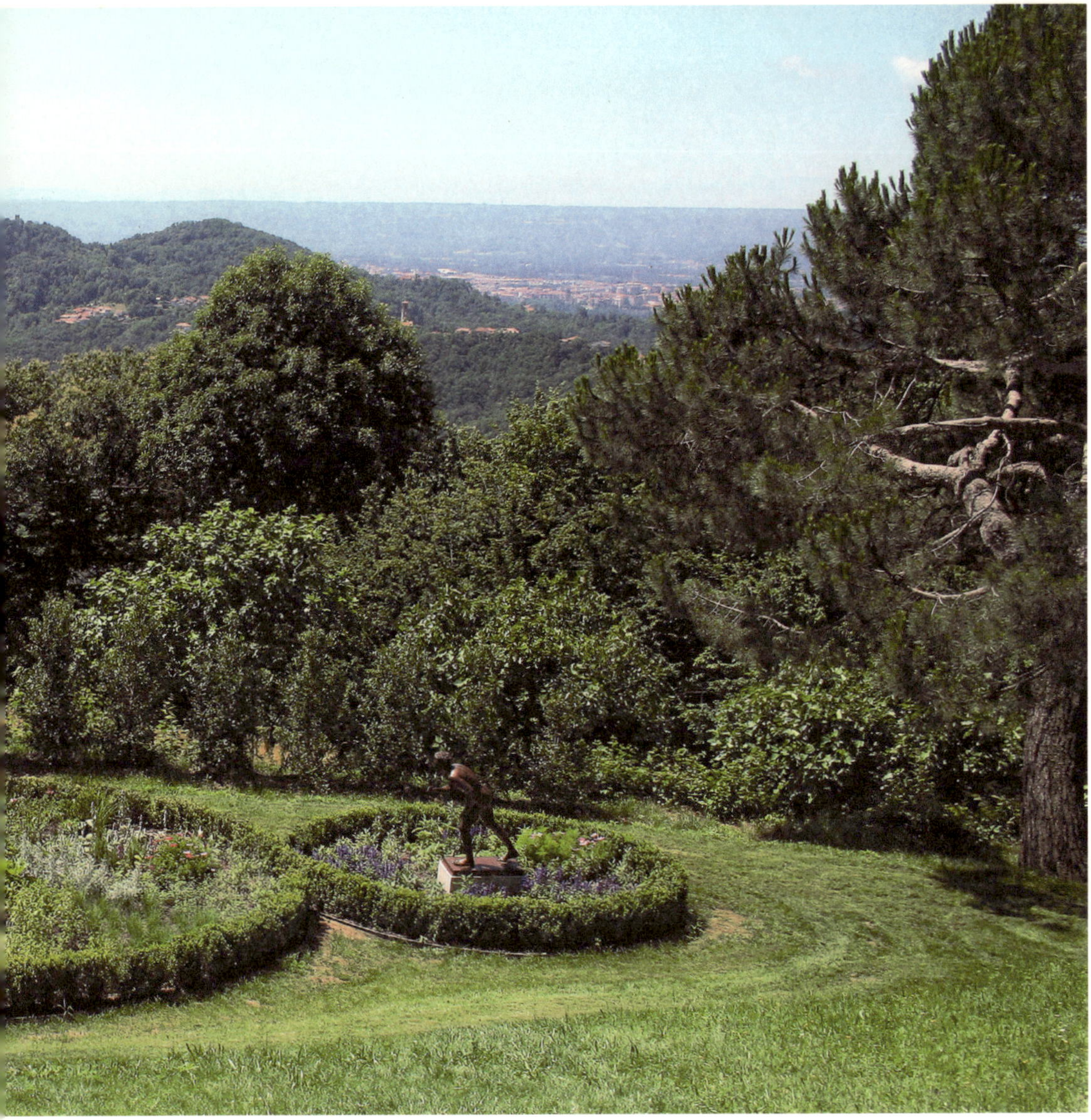

# Third Paradise

It was in March 2003 that Bush and Blair, with the support of many governments, declared preventive war on Iraq.

I found the event deeply upsetting. What was happening was the climax of a folly that involved the entire human race. It was the last straw of "political" perversity that broke the back of history, a worldwide aggression that came on top of a series of conflicts, of monstrous aggressions.

On television and in the newspapers I saw people all over the world coming out into the streets and filling the squares to say "that's enough!" To say "no." Humanity had come out into the open, exposing itself physically, knowing that it had no other power. In those moments I had a clear perception that the silent demonstration by the population of the world which I was watching could be considered, although it was far from being recognized, as the first worldwide vote. It was an expression of democracy that embraced the planet. How could it be ignored? How could one fail to join in with such a spontaneous, extraordinary movement? How could one avoid responding to that heartfelt appeal by the whole world?

In reality the events that were taking place were not exclusively a question of politics, but brought the entire history of humanity to a day of reckoning.

Behind the demand for change there was, in fact, the necessity for a profound transformation of society. All the cultural deformities inherited from the past were coming to the surface: the very concept of preventive war brought up the impelling need to counterbalance it with the idea of preventive peace. Over the course of history peace has always followed war and has been considered a result of it: thus war has been concealed under the mask of peace and peace has consisted of mere appearances.

In that moment I realized that I myself, notwithstanding my artistic, intellectual and practical commitment to a responsible transformation of society, had to take another, even more decided and effective step to contribute to the change that humanity was silently and desperately pleading for. This is how the symbol of the Third Paradise was born.

In June 2004, during the lecture I gave at Turin University on the occasion of my being awarded a honorary degree in political sciences, I announced the project of the Third Paradise. It was the right place and time to publicly launch an initiative that, starting out from the creativity of art, reacted to the political emergencies which we faced, along with the grave problems that affected every other area of social life.

Aware of the symbolic function of art, I decided to propose a symbol that could serve as a guide on the path toward a new stage of civilization. I conceived the symbol of the Third Paradise as a compass that would indicate the direction to be followed.

What I had in mind was a sign that would be at once a reference to the past, a consideration of the present and a projection into the future. The mathematical symbol for infinity, composed of an unbroken line that forms two circles, permitted this synthesis. In one circle is inscribed the most remote past, the time when the human being was totally integrated with nature, while the other circle can be identified with the second phase of the past, the one in which humanity disengaged itself from nature in a process that has led to the artificial world in which we live today. Artifice and art have the same root: the term "artifact" indicates something "made with art." Alongside the marvelous advances achieved with modern progress, catastrophic conditions that threaten the survival of the human race have also been created. At this critical juncture art must assume the basic responsibility for the human dalliance with the artificial. A very strong pressure is being focused in the present, due to the tension, which has grown exponentially over the last century, between the natural and the artificial sphere. I felt the need to liberate the crucial point that links the two

circles from that pressure by opening a third circle: an area ready to accommodate future time.
Out of this has come the "new sign of infinity," symbol of the Third Paradise. From the central circle, as in a mother's womb impregnated by the two earlier paradises, the natural and the artificial, the new humanity is born.
I would like to make it clear that the choice of the term "paradise" is not connected with the religious concept of transcendence, but with an ideal of life on this Earth.
The ancient Persian root of the word "paradise" signified "walled garden," a place filled with life and protected from the aridity of the surrounding desert. In ancient history we continually encounter marvelous gardens: from Herodotus's and Strabo's accounts of the hanging gardens of Babylon to the splendid remains of Hadrian's Villa at Tivoli. In the Middle Ages gardens were also used for the cultivation for officinal herbs and the production of medicines. Eventually the modern art of the garden assumed territorial connotations: in the Italian, French or English style. However, the underlying idea that characterizes all these places is that of a nature controlled, selected and contained by the artistry of the human being, who through an adequate understanding of botany and geology was able to design the present and future appearance of this microcosm.
During the Age of Enlightenment many of the botanical gardens of monasteries and the ornamental gardens of noble palaces were opened to the public. My idea of a Third Paradise is a revival of the original principle of a garden defended against all surrounding dangers. A garden that today must be identified with the entire planet Earth, wrapped in a thin and fragile layer of atmosphere that constitutes its wall enclosure and protects it from the vacuum of outer space. This planetary garden is the Third Paradise and all human beings have to become increasingly conscious of their responsibility as "gardeners," i.e. as the makers of their own environment.
By this I do not mean that humanity will have to renounce the aspiration to affluence, but it will have to change its way of understanding the paradigms that underlie this concept. Milan Kundera has written with wisdom and intelligence on this, speaking of the difference between well-having and well-being. The first of these has been do-

minant since the economic booms of the 20th century, turning much of the citizenry into schizophrenic and continually dissatisfied consumers. Well-being on the contrary is a condition to which all humanity aspires and one that requires a great awareness of oneself and of one's environment.

It is important to grasp the complexity of the reality in which we live, in order to plan our interventions in such a way as to achieve the best possible results. In the garden, for example, organic material reproduces itself independently without producing waste that has to be disposed of. The tree is nourished by decomposition of the leaves that fall in the autumn, the soil reabsorbs the rotten fruit and lays the foundations for rebirth in the spring. This is something which the people of antiquity summed up in the myth of Adonis, loved for half the year by Persephone, goddess of the underworld and the winter, and for the other half by Aphrodite, the Venus of the Romans, a deity linked to the flowering of spring and the vitality of summer. In 1967 I created a work called the *Venus of the Rags* which has become an icon of recycling, in that she transfuses her own incorruptible beauty into an indistinct mass of garbage and like King Midas, who turned everything he touched into gold, gives it a new splendor.

In today's world, with the production of artificial materials, we have set in motion a process different from the natural one. It is urgent to develop and promote new strategies to reconvert the inorganic waste derived from oil and come up with systems that are able to balance the ratio of gases in the atmosphere–for example oxygen and carbon dioxide–that has been rendered unstable by the continual emission of greenhouse gases as a byproduct of the burning of fossil fuels. An exemplary attempt to establish a new equilibrium is that of the *troço verde* which has been present in the city of Curitiba in Brazil for over thirty years.

The man who devised the project was the city's mayor, Jaime Lerner, who as far back as 1971, in order to solve the problem of the disposal and recycling of waste, had introduced the "trash that is not trash" program. The initiative, aimed at areas of the city with a low-income population, entailed the exchange of sacks of sorted waste ready for recycling for surpluses of seasonal fruit and vegetables, tickets for the public transport system and exercise books for children. This solution allowed the municipality to actively involve people in environmental policies, while reducing the cost of the public service as well. The figures bear witness to the success of the initiative: 34 thousand families have disposed of 11 thousand metric tons of waste, obtaining in exchange 1200 tons of surplus vegetables and a million bus tickets, and 200 tons of waste in exchange for 1,200,000 exercise books. In this case the restoration of the environment has also served to provide the needy with food, increase the use of public transport and distribute educational aids. Such initiatives are still being carried out in certain contexts, despite the fact that Curitiba is a city with a population of over two and a half million. They are interventions that act on specific sectors, but that can have positive effects for the entire community. Experiences like this, if multiplied, could bring about changes of global significance.

So new practices need to be introduced that are capable of organizing the movement of the entire body social in an efficient way. A universal commitment is necessary if we are going to be able to go on turning our gaze on the universe from the Earth, in the awareness that our base will remain this wonderful planet which for the moment has no equals and whose uniqueness must be preserved.

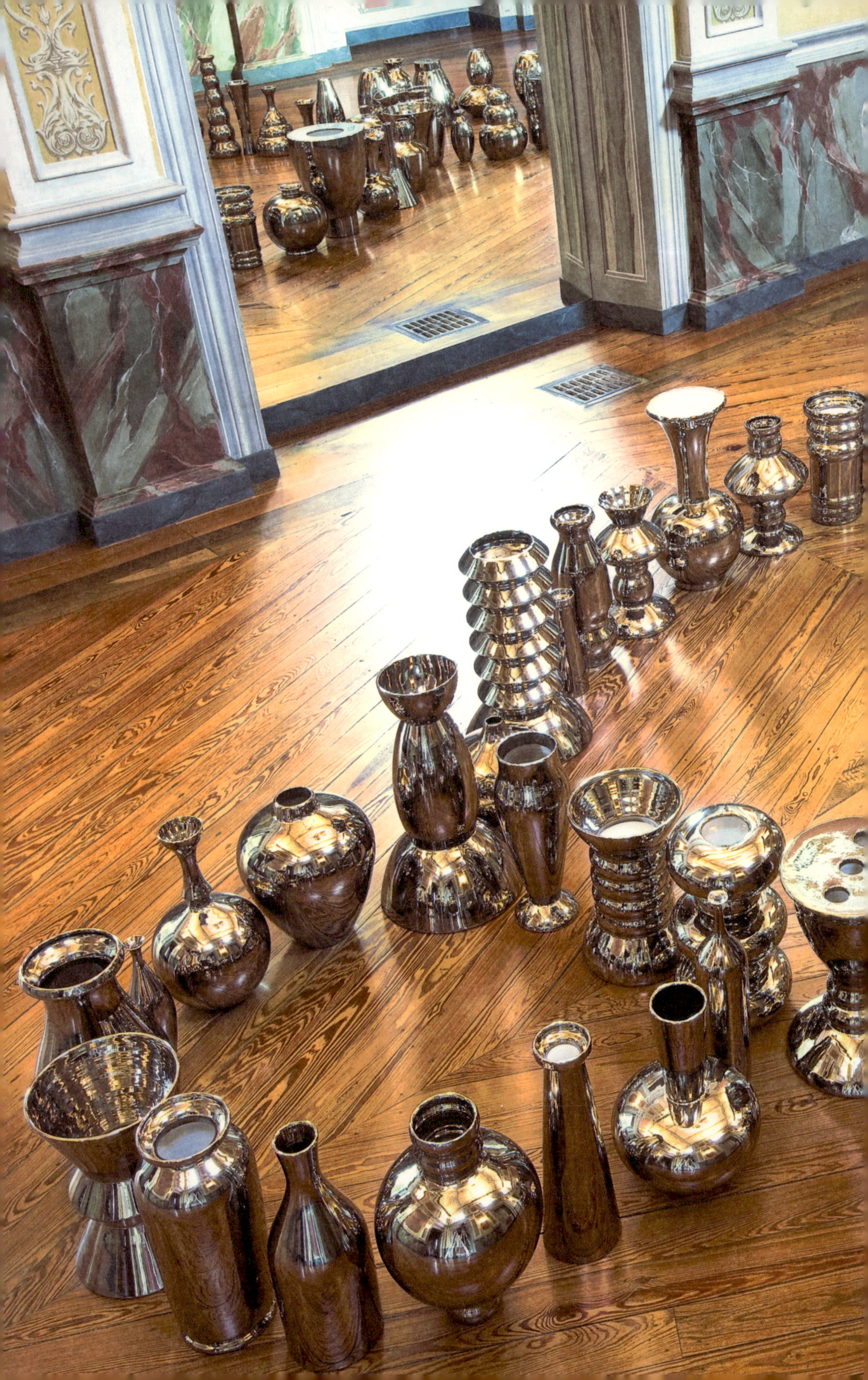

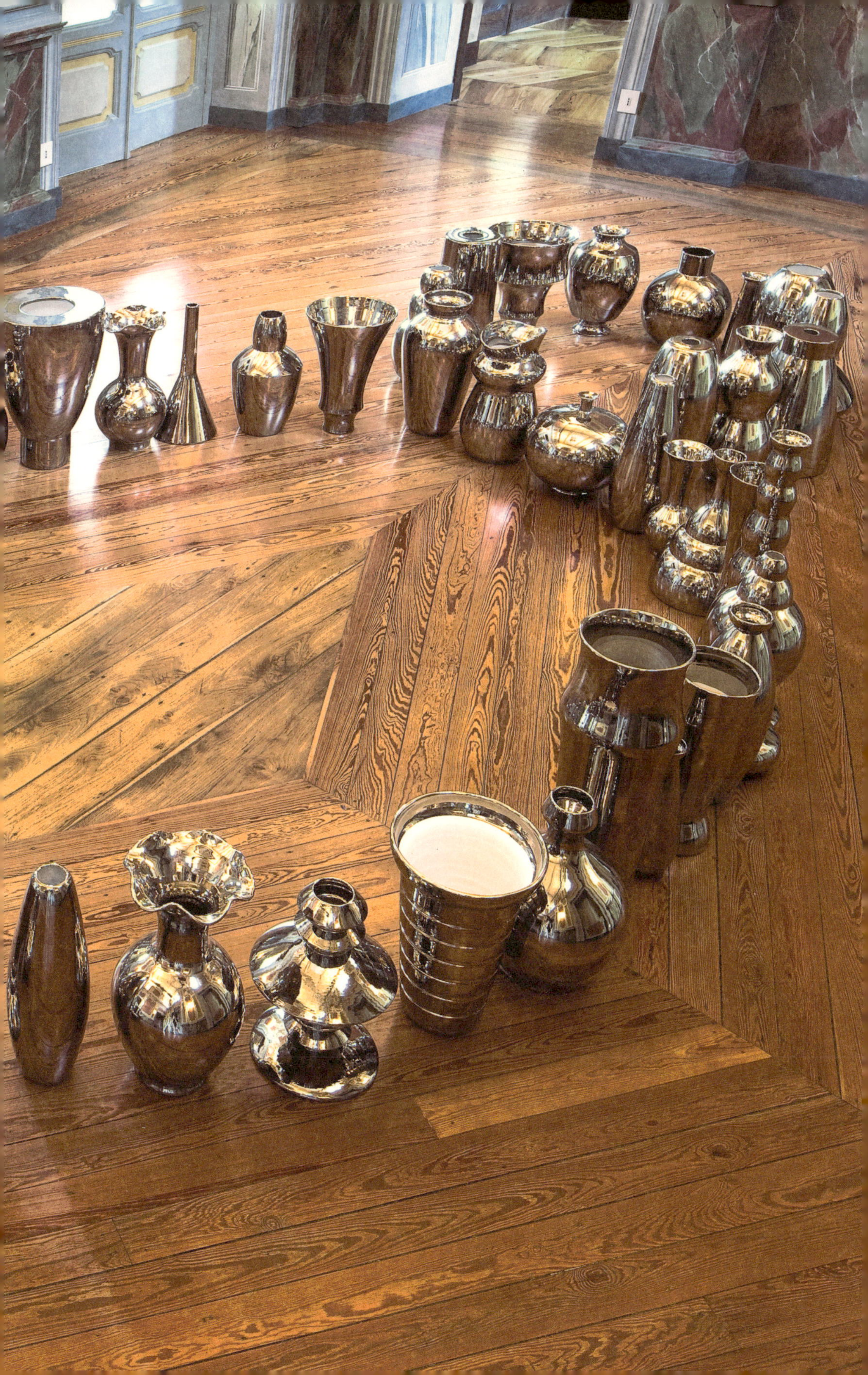

# Wealth as sharing

The idea that humanity in its infancy was completely integrated into nature is taken for granted, and to me seems beyond question. However, the Adamitic idea of a Garden of Eden in which human beings lived off nature without effort, as everything was provided for them, is ingenuous. *Homo sapiens* has faced the same problems of survival as any other species, and if it continues to exist it is due precisely to its ability to manipulate its environment. Even today the "first paradise" can be found in non-anthropized nature, i.e. where human beings have not intervened to modify it to suit their needs. Through ethological and paleoethnological research we can understand how the human race was obliged to interact for millennia with the terrestrial habitat, proceeding with the progressive development of the "second paradise." Moreover, animals in nature act in ways similar to human beings and produce artificial structures. It suffices to think of the hives of bees, the dams built by beavers or the nests of birds. The peculiarity that distinguishes humanity from other creatures is the ability to symbolize what it does. Human beings have lived artificially only since the time when they formed an awareness of that artifice. The capacity to produce is not enough; the true progress achieved by humanity has consisted in giving a symbolic value to the tool it has devised. A stone in the hand of a man or a woman is not just an implement, but also symbolizes the power that derives from the ability to overcome the limitations imposed by the conditions of the environment.

Thus as time passed the concepts of artifice and power have been fused culturally. It must be pointed out and emphasized, however, that certain groups of human beings, for a variety of reasons, have not gone down the same road as those who have gradually exercised their capacity for control not just of the environment, but also of other human beings.

Coming to the modern era, we can see how power has been acquired in the world by those populations who have made use of science and technology to exploit civilizations lacking that knowledge, and how the latter have been ruthlessly subjugated. The countries that have not gone through the modern process of artificial growth have been absorbed and taken advantage of by the systems of the countries that are more "advanced" in the "second paradise." Yet a strong self-criticism has emerged precisely in the industrialized and therefore most economically powerful regions. From this area came Marx with *Das Kapital*, the fundamental text of the Soviet communism that, after overthrowing tsarist rule, held sway in the USSR until its fall in 1989. The reaction against capitalism has shattered and brought down, unfortunately using means of atrocious and brutal violence, the potentates of age-old cultures like that of China. It may seem paradoxical, but we have to recognize that communism has contributed to the success of the current capitalist globalization. It was in "communist" China, in fact, that today's "consumerist" China emerged. Almost all the former communist countries, together with India, South America and some parts of Africa, are now going through the same process as the industrialized countries; we are seeing a uniform extension of Northwestern culture on a global scale. It is quite evident that the last century has brought about an anthropological transformation in the history of the planet perfectly in keeping with the theories of Darwin. And note that I am using the term "transformation" rather than that of "evolution" used by Darwin, which has instead taken on the sense of progressive improvement, assigning a value to this anthropological change.

*previous pages*
*The Third Paradise,*
4th Biennal of Ceramics in Contemporary Art, Madrid, 2010
photo: Enrico Amici

As Gilles Clément rightly argues, the Darwinian vision, in which progress is the result of continual selective pressure through which the stronger and fitter have got the better of the weaker, has been used to legitimize the colonialism of the 19th century and the extreme *laissez-faire* economics of the 20th. Their supporters declared the ever more markedly unequal distribution of wealth between poor and rich countries to be evidence of an inevitable and scientifically incontestable selection. Thus in the manual of the Hitler Youth we find traces of an evolutionary fundamentalism that states: "we mold the life of our people and our laws in conformity with the dictates of genetics." Today science and even the market are reassessing the trust put in Darwin's ideas and rediscovering the writings of Lamarck, who came up with a theory by which change is the result not just of a macro-adaptation to environmental conditions, but also of an individual micro-dynamics aimed at overcoming the difficulties present in that individual's ecosystem; and thus in the human sense the personal capacity to intervene in the situation. So the individual is not impotent in the face of great systems that are modified over the course of historical periods far longer than the life cycle of the human being, but can bring about a change in the community at a personal level and even, as a consequence, within his or her own existence. We realize that reality is the product of a relativity so widespread that it touches the minimum and the maximum dimensions. Personal initiative can generate a society founded on subjective responsibility rather than on an ideological creed. Hence the recognition of each individual identity leads to the composition, by correlation, of the mosaic of the communal identity. At this point it has to be asked in what way can we shape a human community in which the specific individuality of each person is recognizable? A chaotic use of the personal will that leads to the most extreme individualism and results in nihilism, i.e. in total nullification of that community, is certainly not to be desired. And yet, in the absence of fear, it is possible to ascend from nihilism to the construction of a organized structure.

As an artist I have seen that nullification in the mirror: it is a nothing, however, full of everything. The mirror is nothing because it does not exist without something to reflect. So I assigned to this absence of content the numerical value of zero and decided to divide the mirror in half, to make it reflect itself through its double, thereby passing from zero to two. By means of this division I began to multiply the mirror: splitting it in two and progressively shifting the halves so that they formed an angle on the axis of their division, the mirrors are multiplied by reflecting each other. In this way the two progenitor mirrors can be reproduced *ad infinitum*. This virtual process achieved with the mirror corresponds exactly to the biological one of cellular subdivision. Dividing, the cell is multiplied by two, initiating a process of proliferation. The cells differentiate and organize themselves until the human body is completely formed. From this process I have deduced the foundation on which to base the social law that I call sharing, or *condivisione* in Italian.

It is clear that multiplication stems from division and, being a consequence, cannot be considered a principle. The principle can be identified, in fact, in the division, which in the social sense finds expression as *condivisione*, "dividing with" or sharing. The consequences of starting out from this principle are the spread of wellbeing and prosperity to the entire human community. In "con-division" the wealth of each person is the wealth of all and the wealth of all can be enjoyed by each individual. If we take, instead, multiplication as the principle of social economics, as has been done up to now, the wealth of physical and immaterial resources is reduced to an individualistic and exclusive accumulation. By contrast a society that develops on the basis of the concept of division produces wealth that is not exclusive and can be enjoyed by all. The mirror can certainly be subdivided into pieces with different shapes, as we see when it shatters. These shapes can be put back together again like in a jigsaw puzzle. Each fragment of the mirror, like each piece of the puzzle, coincides with the always different shapes of the units that are located around it. The line that unites all the different forms into a single vision is the line of "con-division." Each person, therefore, is in him or herself society and has to be aware of and participate in every function that concerns that society. In my view this could be taken as a formula for democracy.

The democratic republic, as it has developed in the countries of the Northwest, can be seen as the best form of government, since it tends to metabolize conflicts internally. All this reflects a continual tendency towards an ameliorative change in the relationship between individual and society. In any case change is in itself an unavoidable phenomenon. As Heraclitus put it: "Nothing is permanent except change." However, a distinction has to be made between changes of short and long duration: the latter are characterized by a marked persistence in time and history. The situation demands, without doubt, a change of the first type, i.e. as rapid as possible.

Extensive structures like religious, political and economic and financial systems, which have come into being through a long process of formation and organization, turn into gigantic autonomous bodies whose ideals cannot be separated from the resources on which they feed, and so allow them to survive. Any change in ideals would put a strain on the organization of these structures and their procurement of economic resources that are intended to keep those ideals alive, to the point turning them into a pretext for that very procurement. Machiavelli wrote: "It must be remembered that there is nothing more difficult to plan, more doubtful of success, nor more dangerous to manage than the creation of a new system. For the initiator has the enmity of all who would profit by the preservation of the old institutions and merely lukewarm defenders in those who would gain by the new ones." In the epoch-making passage that we are facing many traditional values are being undermined and it has become necessary to look to a transformation of global proportions that requires profound modifications of our way of thinking and acting. This change will inevitably affect the interests of the systems referred to above. Taking these inescapable factors into account, it appears evident that the transition to a new era of human society can only take place by producing ideals capable of absorbing the old ones, even in economic terms. To bring about this transformation lukewarm defenders are not enough. The commitment of the entire human community is needed, commencing with intellectuals, thinkers and people who, like artists, can exercise their freedom and translate it into practical responsibility.

All the critical positions that are presented for public debate today should be carefully considered, for it is out of denunciation that new proposals are born.

I do not want to be part of a purely critical process, but am looking for signs, means and practices that respond to existing problems and can lead to a responsible social transformation that we call the Third Paradise. It is a search for proposals that are never absolute but can be checked against the effectiveness of their results. Criticism is important, but it is not sufficient. The intellectual energy lavished on it needs to be translated into a competitive effort to produce new values; here competition is not meant in the sense of vying with others in order to win or lose, but in that of its etymological root *cum petere*, which signifies "to go together," "to seek together." "Competition" becomes "con-division." In this dividing with, what I am able to do for the community I do for myself. In this sense altruism is the most egotistic behavior that can be imagined. If I take care of the life around me, I am in fact the first to benefit from it.

We must be careful, however, not to confuse the principle of con-division with egalitarianism and imposed uniformity. I stress once again that we have a ruinous example of this in communism, at least as we experienced it in the 20th century. It was a system that crushed the creative potential of the individual and stifled direct exchange between people. As a result it blocked the economic and productive dynamics that flows from the multiplicity of human initiatives. Communism in power created a mass of workers with a single boss, an absolute accumulation of property through a dogmatic idea in which everything was prearranged by an indisputable supreme will.

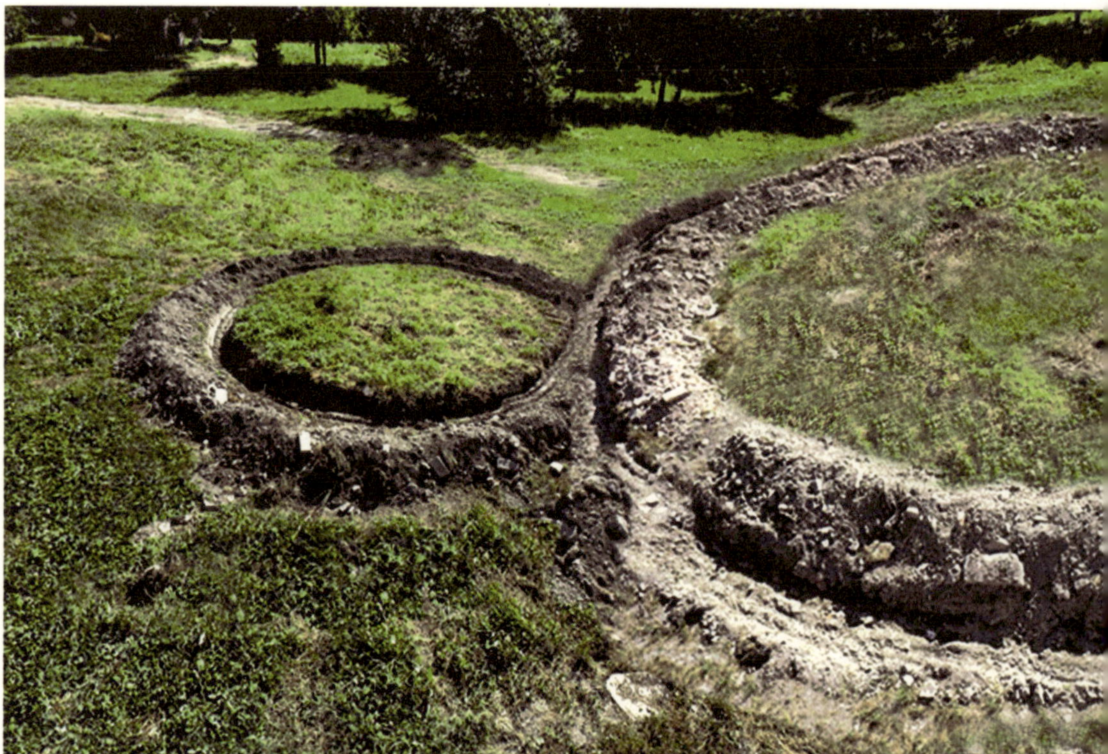

*The Third Paradise Furrow*,
Venice, *51st International*
*Art Exhibition*,
Isola di San Servolo,
Venice, 2005
photo: Claudio Abate

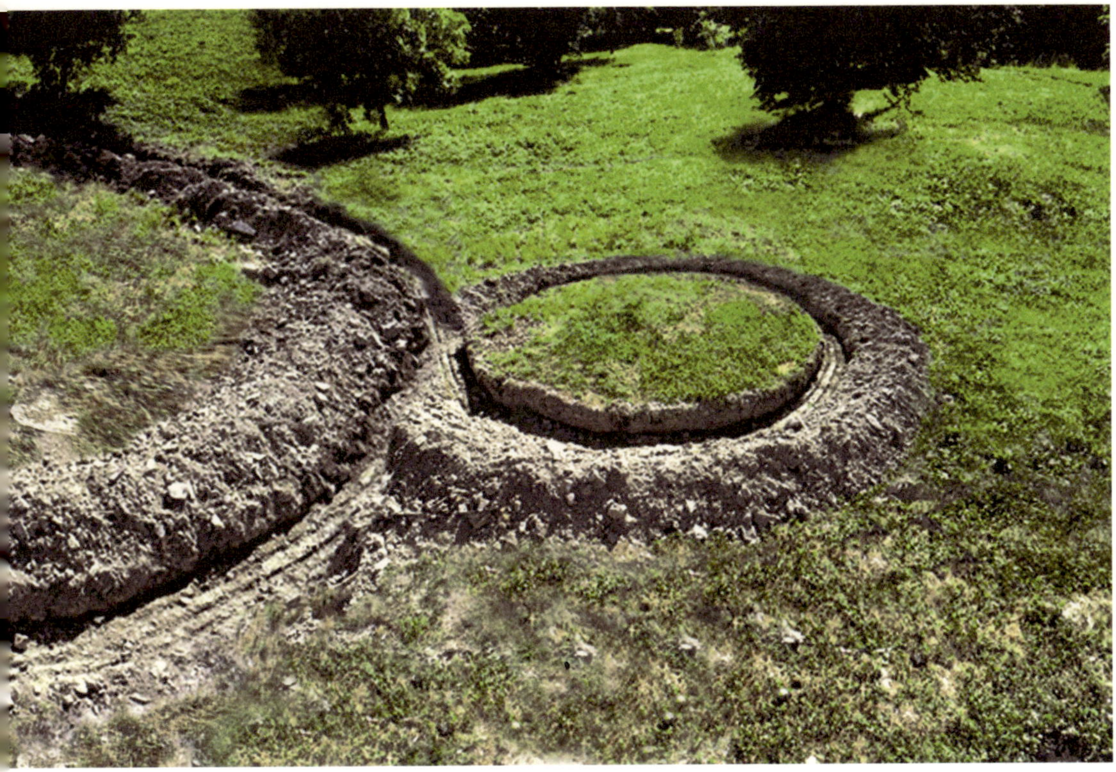

# Sustenance as production and trade on a global scale

Capitalism, to which there seem to be no alternatives today, has to be transformed, by assuming molecular and diffuse forms, in order to favor the processes that regulate, at a universal level, a healthy and balanced social organism. Let us take the concept of money as an example. Money should be seen as something that serves as a means like other units of measurement: like the meter, the kilogram or the liter. The lack of a balanced relationship between currencies permits the more technologically advanced countries to give their own currency a higher purchasing power, thereby creating a marked inequality with regard to the countries from which they get their raw materials. As a result the currencies of these countries lose so much value that the local communities are unable to make use of the products that are the fruit of their labor. Even the raw materials extracted in this way assume a cost that is prohibitive for the countries from which they come. In addition there is no possibility of their economic development because the production and sale of any marketable commodity for local use are politically thwarted.

The circulation of money can be compared to the circulation of blood: both have to be regulated by a general system. Trading currency is the glucose that allows energy to be distributed all over the body. The function of the economy on the other hand can be likened to that of the liver; when toxic substances are taken in the role of the liver is to absorb them, becoming ill to defend the body itself. When the toxicity of financial speculation exceeds the hepatic function's capacity of absorption, catastrophic situations develop that affect the whole social organism. Our society's liver is increasingly under strain and the lack of monetary glucose in vast areas of the planet is causing necrosis of the tissue of the international community.

Now what is a healthy body, understood in the sense of the body social?

A healthy body has a brain that is able to regulate the organism because it has an awareness of the whole. For example bulimia, both as a disturbance in the eating behavior of the individual and as a metaphor for modes of social behavior, is the manifestation of an imbalance that stems from a lack of awareness of the organism's needs and limits. Anorexia, on the other hand, is the inability to reconcile the mind with the requirements of its body, leading the will to take the place of any vital function: a disorder that can culminate in death. In society bulimia manifests itself as the continual stimulus to consume products and regurgitate them immediately in the form of garbage. Anorexia is the kind of financial speculation that distances the economy from its organic operation, leading to the emergence of that pernicious vacuum of which we are now all too well aware.

Social organization, like a brain, has to understand what the real functions of the body are and reconcile them with the initiative of the mind itself.

Each individual has a twofold need: sustenance and the production that is required to ensure it. Today sustenance is no longer just a matter of hunting and farming, but is increasingly linked to a mental state. Even those who devote themselves to conceptual works are carrying out a productive activity and have the same rights as those who are directly engaged in the production of material sustenance. The extreme growth curve of intangible production has led, however, to a reversal of the situation, with a consequent disparity in rights and an increase in injustice. What is needed is a real equivalence between the demand for products and their production at the local and global level. Systems of minimal economics, such as the provision of microcredit, can benefit sections of humanity that live in a state of great insecurity and counterbalance the great systems of speculation; just as the short supply chain–which reduces the superstructures of both production and finance–stimulates initiative and trade at the local level, often alienated by the major systems. If the latter are capable of conditioning initiatives in the industrialized countries, they create situations of even greater dependence and subjection in the poorest countries on Earth; in these, in fact, there is very little autonomy in the processes of exchange between production and use, since both work and the value of money are exclusively constrained by the policies of big foreign companies.

Globalization is a phenomenon of our time, characterized by macro-production and macro-economics. The tendency is to consider progress as the response to a collective desire for growing artificial prosperity, continually fed, notwithstanding the current imbalance between situations of unbridled consumption and total indigence, by the need to have more consumers.

This drive requires an increase of energy that goes hand in hand with the overproduction of goods. However much talk there may be of the risks of global collapse inherent in growth, we still see governments clinging to this concept of progress that demands an exponential rise in the consumption of all natural resources, geared to the great expansion of the modern way of life.

The Italian art of the 20th century has been implicated in the phenomenon of modernity through two contrasting movements, one of growth, the other of de-growth: futurism in the first part of the century and *arte povera* in the second.

The futurist current expressed with vigor the impetus of an avant-garde that was pushing the entire society toward a future of freedom ready to welcome progress as a conquest without end. It celebrated the thrill of speed in the velocity of automobiles, aircraft and trains, glorified the smoke of chimneys and dreamed of cities glittering in the whirl of electric lights. At that time there were just a few, slow vehicles on the roads were and prop-driven airplanes were making their first ventures into the skies. Certainly no one imagined the launch of missiles and the dropping of atomic bombs–both of which were to occur before the middle of the century–and nor could it have been predicted that automobiles would invade the cites, reducing them at times to paralysis. The postwar economic boom gave new impetus to the euphoria of modernity, as the skyscrapers of New York gleamed in the night and the affluence promised by the system of consumption appeared to be within the reach of all. In the sixties the *arte povera*

or "poor art" movement was born in Italy; the term "poor" reflects a quite different approach to the fervor of futurism and the clamor of consumerism, in that it perceives the sense of saturation reached by an ideal of growth that has given its best. *Arte povera* distanced itself from the bulimic opulence of industrialized society and concentrated on an organic essentiality. It stripped itself of the superfluous, immersing itself in elementary processes and becoming the linchpin of a shift in perspective that reclaimed both the responsibilities not assumed in the past and the opportunities not seized. For this reason the very term "poor" can even be regarded as a precursor of the economic concept of "de-growth," put forward in 1974 by Nicholas Georgescu-Roegen in his theories of ecological economics. As the name suggests, this is an economics based on ecological principles, in contrast to the one that governs systems relying on economic growth. In accordance with these principles it is obvious that de-growth should not be understood solely in terms of economics, but also in those of environmental sustainability. In this connection people are talking once again of nuclear power as a clean source of energy, a subject that is still the focus of great debate among scientists. Carlo Rubbia, winner of the Nobel Prize for Physics in 1984, says "[...] not only are oil and the other fossil fuels running out, but uranium too is destined to grow scarce over the next 35-40 years [...]. So we cannot go on drawing up plans for energy on the basis of erroneous predictions that threaten to take us down the wrong track. We have to develop the most important source of energy that nature has always placed at our disposal, without limits and at zero cost: the sun that illuminates and warms the Earth every day." As far as nuclear power is concerned, he points to the possibility of using "thorium, an element widely available in nature, to fuel a nuclear amplifier. This is an accelerator, a non-critical reactor, in other words one that does not set off chain reactions [...] you can't make a bomb out of thorium. In this way the link between the military nuclear industry and the civil one would be broken for good."
Setting aside the continuing scientific commitment to research into the possibilities of atomic energy, let us imagine what form our approach to the supply of energy might take in the future. There are two courses that can be taken: the first concerns the effort to make progress in the utilization of alternative and clean energy–from solar

to wind to geothermal–and other sources that are yet to be explored and to halt the consumption of mineral sources and the pollution of the soil and the atmosphere; the second concerns the activation of processes of sustainability on a widespread level, through the local development of real attention to the daily choice of the energy we use.
Sources of alternative energy have been criticized on the grounds of the aesthetic impact that they have on the landscape. In my view wind turbines are not only of value for their utility, but can also be seen as sculptural works of our time: they sprout like gigantic flowers in our landscape, just as solar and photovoltaic panels shine in the sun, creating a new urban panorama that can be compared to a work of art. Any one of our homes could be taken as a paradigm of this technological transformation. Today the majority of the houses in which we live require a very high consumption of energy, impacting strongly on our health, on the environment and on the economy. The technologies at our disposal already permit us to save a lot of energy on the one hand, and to produce energy on the other. This is possible now in both the industrialized countries and the developing ones. It is a matter of daily choices that the citizen can make for him or herself. In Germany experiments have been made with the *PassivHaus*, a dwelling built with insulation capable of reducing the annual consumption to 15 kilowatt hours per square meter instead of the national average of 220, and in Northern Europe with carbon-neutral houses, whose energy needs are met directly from renewable sources and in which consumption is limited by adequate insulation and by highly efficient electrical appliances. The spread of these systems now needs to be encouraged through the awakening of public opinion.
The reduction of consumption at the local level goes perfectly with the concept and practice of the short supply chain and zero food miles, which entail the use of food produced in the region in which you live, acquired directly from local farmers who follow principles of biosustainability. This cuts down on the expense and the pollution due to transport and brings people back into contact with the seasonal cycles of nature, fostering a greater responsibility in daily choices at the individual and community level. The concept of the short supply chain envisages methods that reduce the utilization of energy and increase the autonomy of local people from every point of view. The aim of

this is not to increase the isolation of the community, but to establish a system on a vast scale that functions thanks to local dynamics: a micro-operation that significantly brings down energy consumption and curbs its waste.
All this determines a synergic relationship between the local and the global, one that becomes manifest in the use of the internet in a symbolic and practical dimension: being present in a precise physical place and at the same time being everywhere on the web.
Zygmunt Bauman has described glocalization as a constant attention to the individual, to the human being and to the local material and immaterial heritage of people and groups, a vision in which the local community is regarded as the foundation of global society.

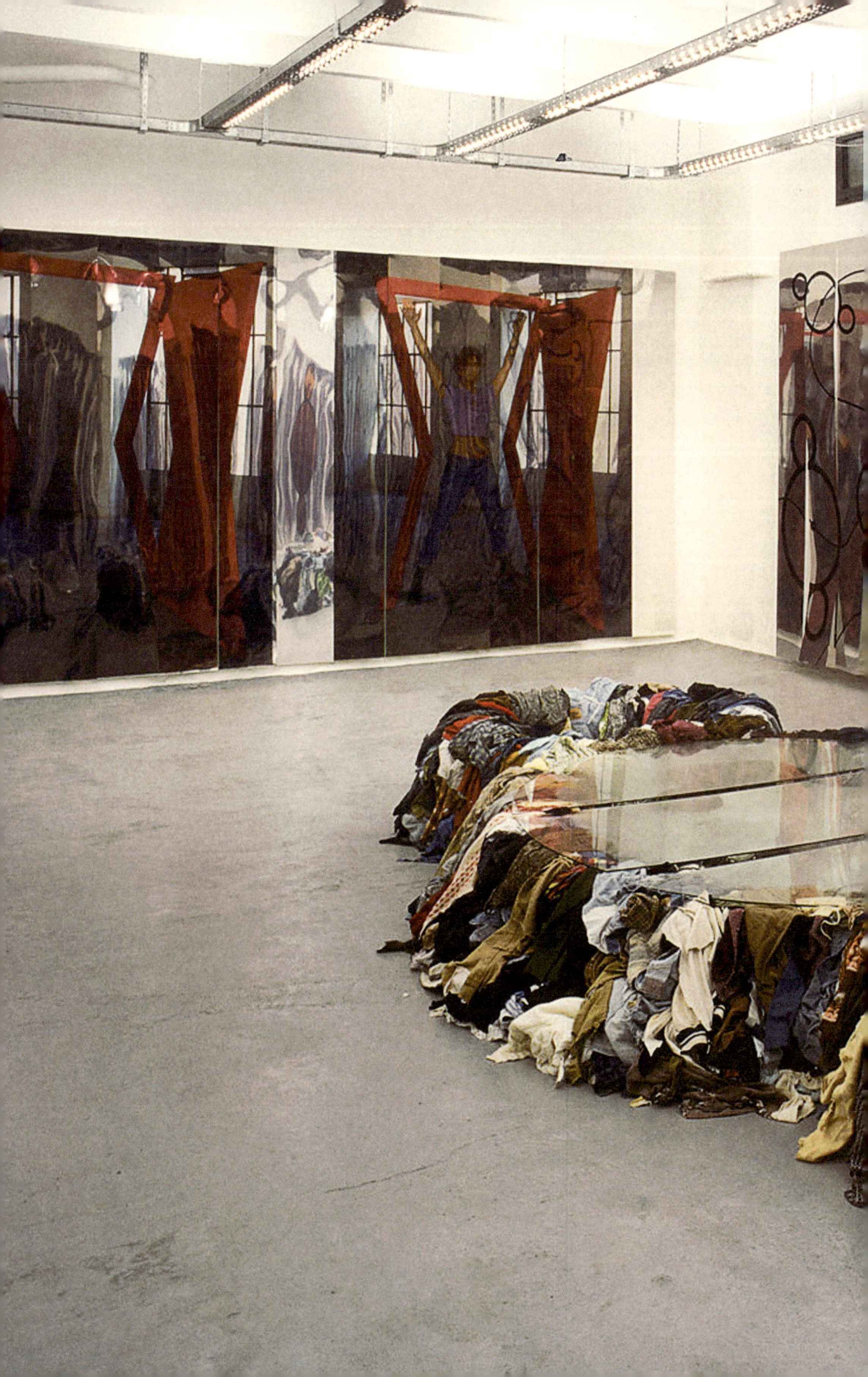

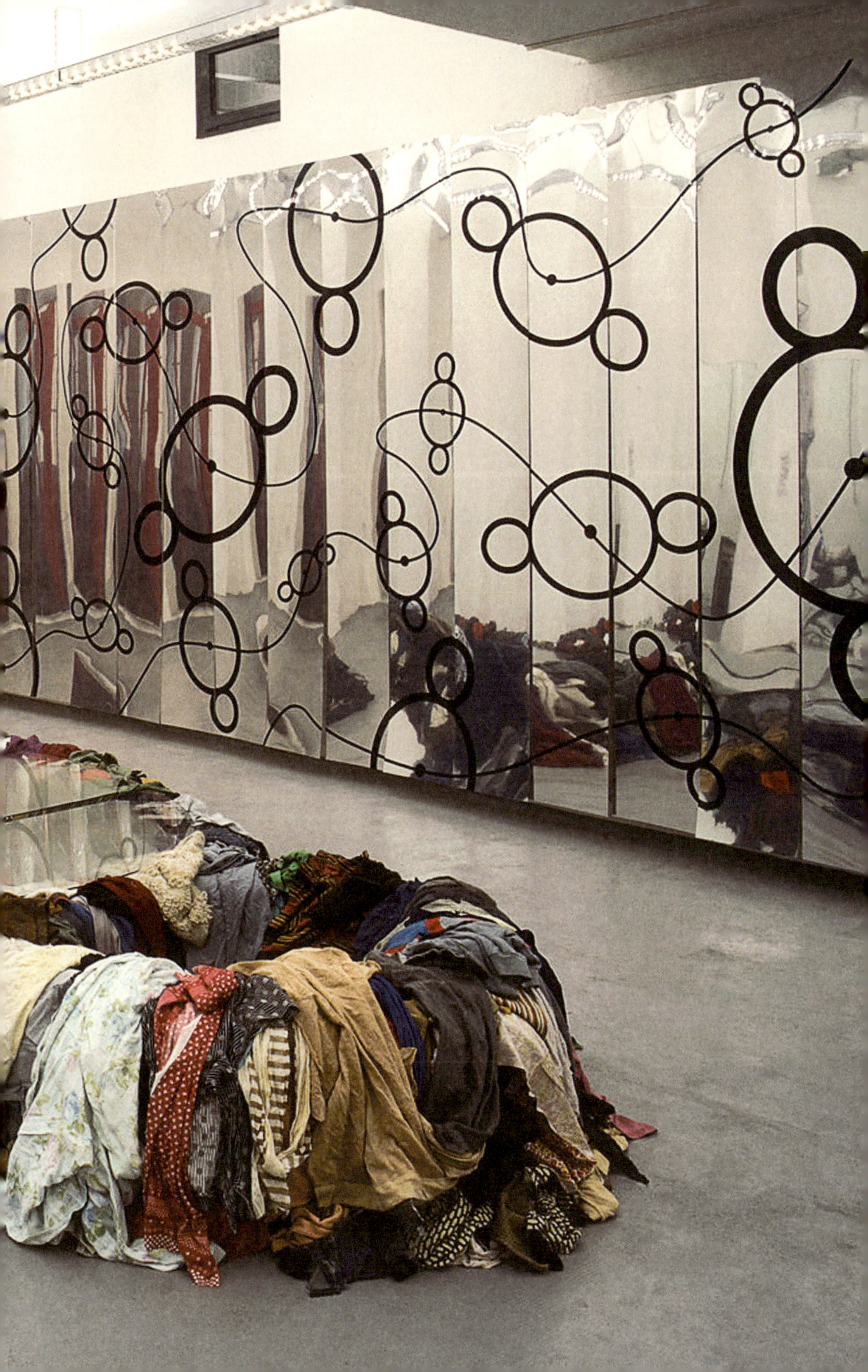

# Survival as population control

In the Paleozoic era an order of mollusks with red shells, called ammonites, had spread through all the seas since they had the ability not just to live underwater, but also to expel water from their shells and thus rise or descend. Their success with respect to other forms of life led them to reproduce until they saturated their environment and went extinct. The red color of their shells is still visible today in the geological strata of the Earth.
Examples of similar phenomena can also be found in human history. For instance the large stone statues that we see today on Easter Island are the visible trace of the passage of a population that died out following the total deforestation of that land. The source of life on the island was in fact the very trees that were sacrificed for the transport and erection of those totems, symbols of political and religious power. These are two cases–one taken from the natural world, the other from the anthropized and ideologically structured world–whose result was the same: total extinction. In the first the end was due to the uncontainable growth of the species, in the second it occurred as a result of the iniquitous exploitation of nature for the construction of symbols of artifice. In today's world these two factors are combined: the unbounded reproduction of human beings and the consumption of natural resources for the progressive growth of the artificial product. And the prospect is that of a growing risk of the extinction of our species. To tackle the problem at the root it is necessary to develop a policy of containment in every area of society. In the first place we need to find the courage to deal with the problem of the proliferation

of human beings on the Earth: to find a way to reduce both birthrates and levels of consumption and at the same time to develop technologies that take advantage of nature without destroying it. We cannot ignore the fact that, despite the slight decline in the rate of growth that began in the eighties, the population of the Earth will continue to increase to a level where it is predicted to reach a point of collapse in the not too distant future.

All the precautions that we are adopting today and the changes that we are making in order to live in an environmentally sustainable way may be thwarted by an abnormal growth of the population. It is possible that a drastic reduction in human numbers may be brought about by epidemics or natural disasters, but this is hardly something to be hoped for. Since the problem exists and we cannot expect it to solve itself, we need to look at all the measures that could be taken to tackle it.

*previous pages*
Michelangelo Pistoletto, Gianna Nannini, *The Third Paradise*, bunkerart, Milan, 2007
photo: Marco Fedele di Catrano

In the North of the world, where socioeconomic affluence has increased, we are seeing a clear drop in the birthrate and so this prosperity can be seen as a limitation of growth. It may appear paradoxical, but in reality wherever there has been a drastic fall in infant mortality, made possible by modern medicine, this has led not just to an increase in life expectancy, but also to a reduction in the number of births. For this reason it is urgent to extend the possibility of benefiting from medical treatments and sustainable technologies for the production of goods and services to countries with a high mortality. In Bangladesh, for example, the reduction in the birthrate has come as an effect of the system of microcredit introduced by the Grameen Bank, founded by Nobel prizewinner Muhammad Yunus. His intervention, in one of the poorest countries on Earth, has promoted economic development and created training and work opportunities especially for women. Yunus has grasped the importance of triggering processes of female entrepreneurship with loans of money, thereby giving women the authority that would otherwise be denied them by the economic and cultural context. Gaining satisfaction not only from the bearing of children, but also from their enterprise, and assuming new responsibilities in the maintenance of the family, women are undoubtedly led to adopt a more prudent attitude toward birth control. It has also been shown that in countries where men devote more time to their children, since their mothers are working, the fertility rate falls to a level close to replacement.

At this point we have to seriously consider the responsibility of the religions in the psychological control of the masses. They are, almost always, egocentric and tend to encourage births in order to increase the number of the faithful who provide them with their legitimacy.

Something similar happens with the consumerist system, which is careful not to speak of de-growth of the population, as less people signifies less consumers. And the intellectuals who spare no pains to convince their fellow countrymen and women to have more children to balance the influx of immigrants are concealing, more or less consciously, an attitude that can be defined as racist. It is, moreover, wholly irrational that moral authorities should still prohibit the use of contraceptives even today, favoring in this way the spread of sexually transmitted diseases and hampering the responsible control of births. Religious leaders have always exercised a strong psychological sway over the sphere of people's sexual behavior.

So much interest on the part of these authorities is symptomatic of the importance of such an intimate, vital and at the same time mysterious area of the human personality, for intense pleasure is hard to rationalize and from this pleasure a new life can come into being. It comes naturally to sublimate this gratification in ideal terms, by placing it at the center of a complex set of thoughts and actions. Sex becomes, in this way, a conjunction between the perception of the intangible and an intense physicality. It turns into a crucial meeting point between the physical and the metaphysical and it is evident that a system of thought that privileges and exalts the metaphysical can condemn and despise the physical.

On the other hand it is not just in the religious field that the phenomenon of sex takes on a central importance, but in the profane one as well. In this sense we are seeing an increasing sexualization of social, economic and political relations; the most obvious example is advertising, which uses it as a means of reaching deeply and in the simplest and most direct way into the private and collective imagination. Nature has given human beings an appetite for both sex and food to ensure the survival and reproduction of the individual. So it is clear that sex can become a commodity, like any object that satisfies desire.

The whole of society is an emotional field continually pervaded by sex, which is not limited to coitus for the purpose of procreation, but reverberates in different types of union that are not necessarily between people of different sexes. If for religion all forms of love not aimed at reproduction should be channeled into the intangible and the divine, in the profane world they are utilized instead for the exaltation of the superfluous; in both cases they translate into speculative practices of power, excessive in character and remote from a balanced relationship between sexuality and social life. Through the exploitation of sexuality it is possible to achieve domination of the mind and its association with feelings of guilt produces morbid excitement, scandal, perversion and depravation.
Bearing in mind the social aspect of population control, our love of our children should be extended in a comprehensive and inclusive manner to all those who are born and enter life. One of the Grameen Bank's statements of fundamental values is: "We shall plan to keep our families small. We shall minimize our expenditures. We shall look after our health." The attention we pay to the wellbeing of our own children becomes at the same time an attention paid to childhood at the social level.
Many argue that where a decline in births takes place, the result is a growing population of the unproductive elderly. Let us look at the facts: on the one hand the increase in the average lifespan as a result of modern medical techniques compensates for the falling number of births; it suffices to think that, in Italy for example, life expectancy has tripled with respect to the beginning of the 20th century. On the other information technology allows the elderly to make themselves useful to society for a very long time, by permitting them to work without muscular effort and physical exhaustion, just as for the young.
Today we increasingly often hear talk of a clash of generations. Frankly it seems crazy to me to argue that there is a conflict between youth and old age, because living longer is an advantage for all. Everyone wishes to live as long as possible. In the past people put their faith in the afterlife because life on the Earth was so short that they were unable to fulfill themselves. Those who did manage to reach a ripe old age were esteemed for the wisdom that their long experience had allowed them to accumulate. Today longevity allows us to achieve an ever gre-

ater awareness, knowledge and fulfillment over the course of our existence. In any case it would be madness to think of getting rid of the old to make room for the young: everyone has a right to life from the moment in which they come into the world. So we have to be rationally aware of the responsibilities we are taking on, from the general perspective of equilibrium, when we decide to have a child. This said, I realize that we are faced with a series of problems that are going to have a greater and greater impact on social security with respect to the relations between the different age groups. On this issue I would like to make a proposal that may appear provocative, but that after all may not be so far-fetched: what is needed is for the elderly to pay a subsidy toward the education of the young. The economy of work ought, in fact, to be readjusted between young and old. The productive activity of the latter, for example, could be extended in time, allowing them to support themselves for longer. This would make it possible to provide grants to the young that would permit them to receive training and to devote themselves to study and research for the development of their own culture. Education and research, in fact, in addition to being essential assets for the individual, are the driving force of society. The possibility of studying for longer would allow the young to make a more gradual entry into productive activity, with the wider range of skills that is necessary to cope with a labor market increasingly based on the idea of mobility. There are still jobs that require physical effort, but the proportion of immaterial professions is constantly growing.

Both the young and the old ought to devote part of their time to activities of social utility and this would also provide them with an opportunity to meet. In the past the family was made up of members of all the different generations and the children, who were raised in part by their grandparents, were fundamental as a workforce for an agricultural and artisan economy. The industrial revolution, from the 19th century onward, has broken down the extended family system by offering each member economic independence. The resulting prosperity has created a situation of alienation in family and generational ties. Today we are faced with the need to build new relationships between people of different ages, while preserving the autonomy of individuals. The experience of cohousing, which originated in Scandinavia, could be a significant example of such interaction. This is based on structures in which a number of people or families live in a residential community with common facilities. The independence of the private home remains guaranteed by personal rooms, but these are supplemented by shared spaces and resources like a library, living room, kitchen, household appliances, workshops, gyms, guestrooms, vegetable gardens, cars, crèches, gardens and the individual skills of the inhabitants. They are generally made up of 20-40 homes of people who have chosen to live together and have decided to share their neighborhood in more participatory and active way. These communities are not based on ideological or religious principles, but on the desire to re-create a lost sociability and to live in a way that has a sustainable environmental footprint and in which running costs can be shared, reducing the expense of daily life. In these places the old and the young are able to share their time, knowledge and projects. In these spaces the creativity of art can be a means of setting in motion common and unifying experiences.

Michelangelo Pistoletto,
Gianna Nannini,
*The Third Paradise*,
Castello Svevo, Bari, 2008
photo: Alessandro
Lacirasella

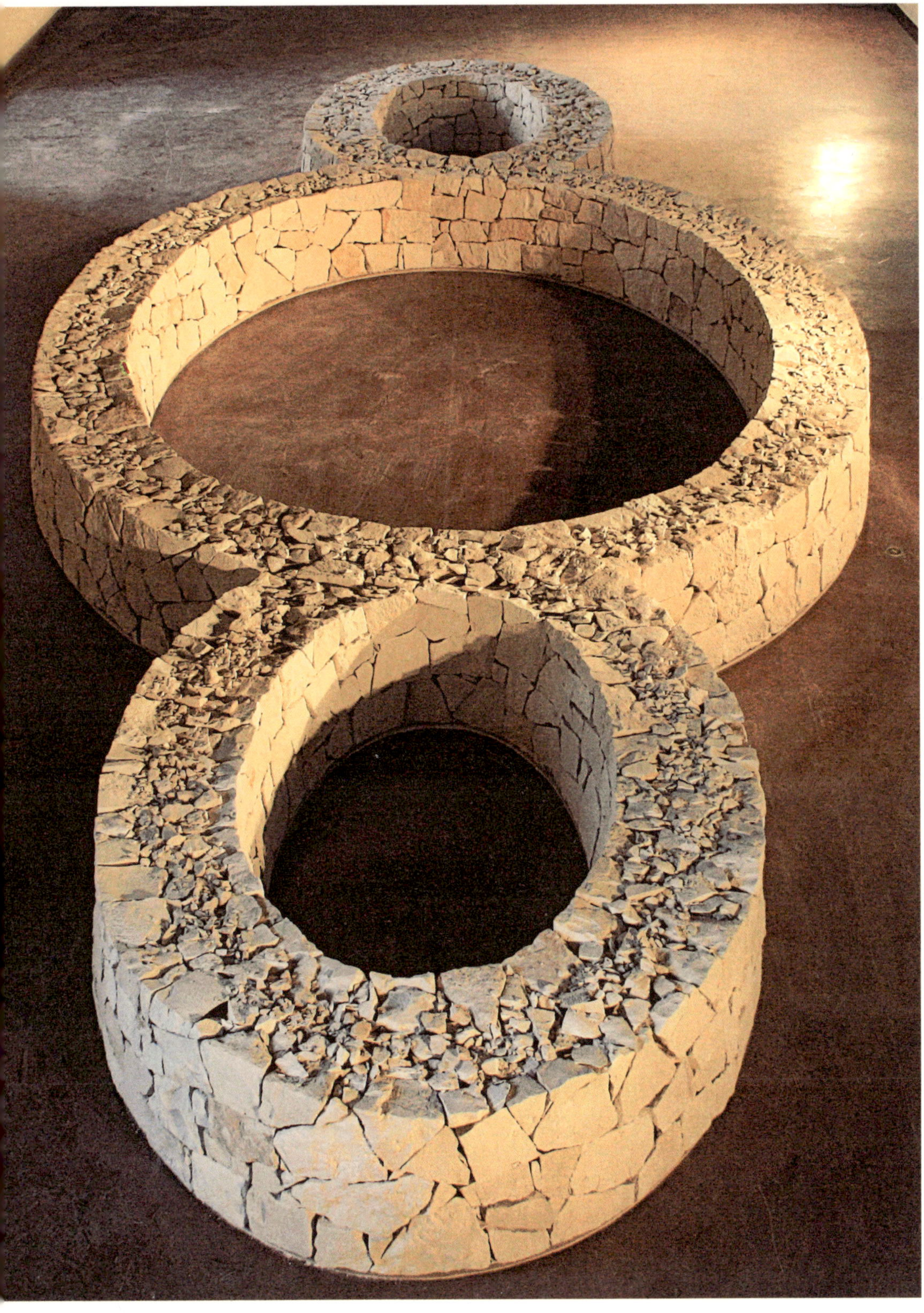

# Education as the primary means of social change

Every society brings up children according to its own ways and customs, but at this moment it is precisely ways and customs that have to change, and to do so profoundly. If there is to be any possibility of openness to change in humanity, this depends primarily on education. We have to accept that we have been shaped by ancient and modern experiences that have to a great extent lost their validity. We have the responsibility, to ourselves above all, to bring about a revolution in education. Devoting ourselves to the education of children means effecting, through their forming, our own transformation as well. The attitude of the individual toward him or herself and toward the community is shaped in the first fifteen years of life. So the theoretical and practical conception of a new society can be totally focused on those fifteen years.

All this makes me believe that with sufficient commitment and attention devoted to the potentialities of the child, change in our society can be brought about at a very rapid pace.

In designing and building computers we are creating a mirror of the human being and this is progressively helping us to understand, in a simplified fashion, the functioning of the human mind. The computer contains an operating system and programs ready to receive and process the data inserted by the user. In the same way a person is born with a program installed that needs to be informed; learning takes place through the input of data into the system that organizes and processes it. Although of recent origin, the history of data processing has gone through a change equivalent to the one that led from the mammoth to today's human being. The first computers were enormous machines that filled entire rooms while carrying out calculations that were still very limited. Gradually a refinement in design has taken place that has made the computer increasingly small as well as complex, to the point where it can now fit into the palm of the hand. In a certain sense it is possible to apply to the computer both the concept of "Darwinian evolution"–in the macro-process of its history–and that of "Lamarckian evolution"–which operates in the micro-dynamics of individual intervention. The human being is at once the computer and its user, but in addition to reflecting the system of the brain the artificial instrument can be used to extend the mental faculties beyond limits that hitherto seemed insurmountable.

Finally we have the possibility of knowing ourselves and we must strive to understand how the education of the child can benefit from this knowledge. There are examples, in the past, of advanced methods, developed by people like Maria Montessori who felt the need to avoid imposing a prepackaged set of notions and offer children instead the opportunity to "learn by doing," by presenting them with sensorial and symbolic materials that allowed continual and direct experimentation.

It is a significant fact that some of the leading figures in the development of information science, such as Jeffrey Bezos, founder of Amazon.com, Sergey Brin and Larry Page, founders of Google, and Jimmy Wales, inventor and founder of Wikipedia, all received a Montessori education. These people have helped to broaden the possibility of interaction between individuals through the web. Out of this has come a new way of reconciling the relations between individual and society; thus education based on these principles prepares the individual to be part of a community that has now assumed planetwide dimensions, in which each person is both independent and a participant.

Looking in the mirror each of us can see every other individual in the same space and at the same time. Personally, as an artist, I have turned the canvas of the picture into a mirror, transforming the solitude of the artist into a self-portrait in which people, looking at their reflections, enter the mirror with me. The mirror picture, in this sense, sums up and symbolizes the relationship between one and all that we find on the internet: in fact the internet can be regarded as a technological version of the mirror picture. In the mirror the phenomenon just described is perceived not just rationally, but also emotionally.

A scientific view of education is not limited, therefore, to the acquisition and utilization of technology. Let's take music for example: it can be transposed mathematically and in this mathematics even the freest and most complex expression of the emotions and imagination is organized and expressed. The imagination leads into the universe of possibilities.

Childhood fantasy is a continual investigation of the possible. As children we begin to fantasize about the world, and this is inevitable. For example, a child does not know what a corkscrew is for, and if it does not see it being used has to provide an answer to the purpose of that object with its imagination; thus the corkscrew becomes a steel ballerina or a drill for finding worms in the ground, and with that play starts. A snowfall is already in itself the direct experience of an event that goes beyond the expected, in that it shows that a multicolored landscape can turn completely white. The child thinks: "if this can happen who knows what other wonders are possible." I remember that at the age of two my father took me in his arms and carried me to the window. It was snowing and I saw the whole garden covered with snow. This sight was so stirring that I still connect snow with that moment. Another powerful emotion from my childhood was the one I experienced when, waking up on Christmas morning, I found some carefully wrapped packages at the foot of the bed. My father had told me that the Infant Jesus (no one had yet heard of Santa Claus in Italy at the time) would come in the night bringing presents. Discovering that it was true filled me with great joy. The child believes everything it is told, especially by the parents who feed and look after it. One Christmas morning a few years later I found a note of thoughtful advice that the Infant Jesus had slipped among the gifts. In those few words appeared a Z with a long stem, just like the one I had seen in my father' handwriting. And so I realized that those presents were from my parents. Remembering that occasion today, I write the Z with a long stem.

Today's schools are the product of the industrial revolution, created with the aim of combating illiteracy and at the same time producing a class of specialized technicians: surveyors and accountants, experts on chemistry, mechanics and electronics, all the way up to the staff of the scientific departments of the university. Apart from a few outstanding exceptions–which do exist in the world–the basic methods of education can still be included in the system of "desk and blackboard." As yet a post-mechanical and postindustrial form of education has not yet come into widespread use and the need is felt for solutions suited to a world of work that on the one hand is becoming increasingly immaterial and on the other requires differentiated activities on the plane of material production, in pursuit of an environmentally sustainable transformation of the planet.

Many teachers feel frustrated because they are asked to operate a mechanism in which they are unable to intervene with means suited to supporting innovative approaches. It is on them that society relies for the acquisition of technical, social and relational skills by the young, but without supplying them with the tools they need for the education of individuals capable of motivating themselves to act and concentrating independently on what they are doing, through an experiential as well as theoretical activity. Methods are required that recognize the fundamental role played by the organization of the educational environment in learning and that permit the exercise of the students' intellectual faculties on interesting and complicated subjects that can reveal and develop all the qualities of the individual. I have personally had the experience of ten years as a teacher in the department of sculpture at the Academy of Fine Arts in Vienna. There it was not a matter of "desk and blackboard," but "hammer and chisel." The task for which I had been brought in was to renew the educational system of that course. The first thing I did was to explain to the students that in my view artistic creation was not exclusively limited to the self-referential system of art, but could interact effectively with every other sector of civil life, and that to do this artistic languages and means provided by advanced technology can also be utilized.

To carry out this activity the course drew on the professional experience of various media, including film, video, performance and music, thereby extending the plastic concept of sculpture to intervention in the environment. Once skills in these fields had been refined, it moved on to investigation of themes related to clothing, food, the design of useful objects and architectural intervention. The students' projects were regularly presented to the public and found expression in artistic interventions in a variety of places, not just the city of Vienna.

With the creation of Cittadellarte in Biella, launched in parallel with my teaching in Vienna, I combined the experience I had gained at the academy with the aims formulated in *Progetto Arte*, the manifesto that I published in 1994 in which I declared: "*Progetto Arte* is based on the idea that art is the most sensitive and complete expression of human thought, and that the time has come for artists to take on the responsibility of establishing ties among all other human activities, from economics to politics, science to religion, education to behavior–in a word, among the threads that make up the fabric of society." Cittadellarte has always had, right from the outset, a strong commitment to education. *UNIDEE*, the University of Ideas, was one of the first initiatives. Its mission is to inspire and bring about a responsible change in society through creative ideas and projects. This approach is the foundation of the whole Cittadellarte project, which has taken the concept of the division of the biological cell as the basis for its subdivision, in turn, into many units, called Uffizi or "Bureaus," corresponding to different sectors of society: education, ecology, spirituality, economics, politics, production, communication, architecture, fashion and nutrition. Art constitutes the reagent that, playing an active part in the fabric of social life, radiates the energies needed to bring about the transition toward a new stage of civil life. The entire activity of Cittadellarte constitutes an active principle for the substantive formation of the Third Paradise. In my view each person should embark on a program of self-education, bearing in mind the suggestions that come from people, groups and institutions that have already taken the road of responsible activation. For a change to take place in a short space of time through an appropriate education of children, it is necessary for adults to try to operate feeling themselves to be children too, since in this way they will be able to accelerate the pace of that change and work on its attainment together with the younger generations. In this light it is interesting to consider the Suzuki method of teaching music which requires the presence and active participation of the parents. As a result they learn alongside their children.

*following pages*
*The Third Paradise*,
Cittadellarte Fashion - Bio Ethical Sostenible Trend, Biella, 2009
photo: Enrico Amici

In countries where access to primary education for all is more difficult, an effort is being made to distribute inexpensive computers for children. This operation not only makes the younger generations computer literate, but fosters a process of education that spreads out from the children to the adults.

Another example we might take is that of the educational departments of museums of modern and contemporary art. The activity they carry out with young people on a daily basis generates in them an interest that is spontaneously transmitted to their parents, who are thereby persuaded to approach and appreciate an art that normally many of them would consider difficult.

The fact is that if we wish to construct a grownup society at last it is necessary to start from the infancy of a new collective consciousness.

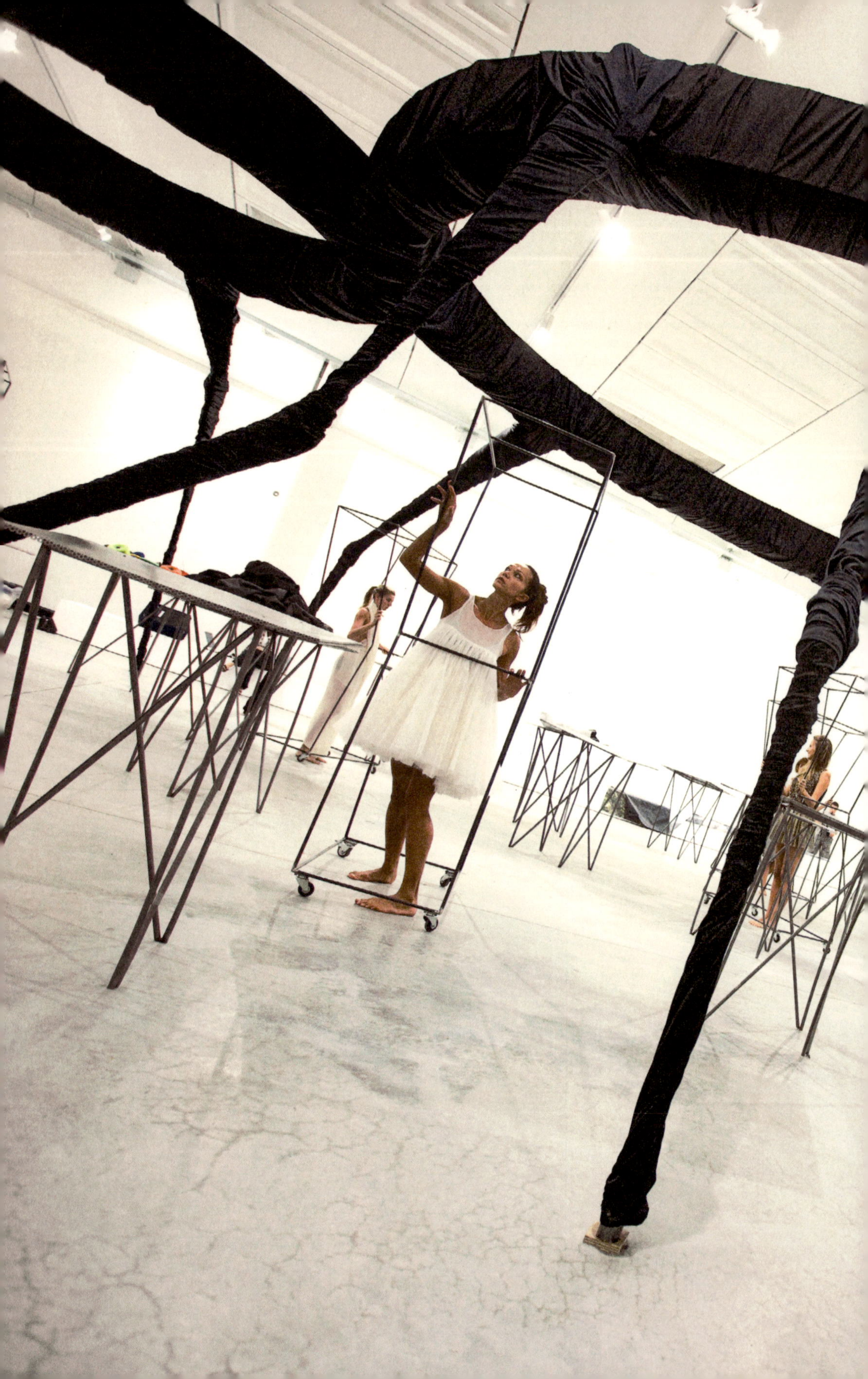

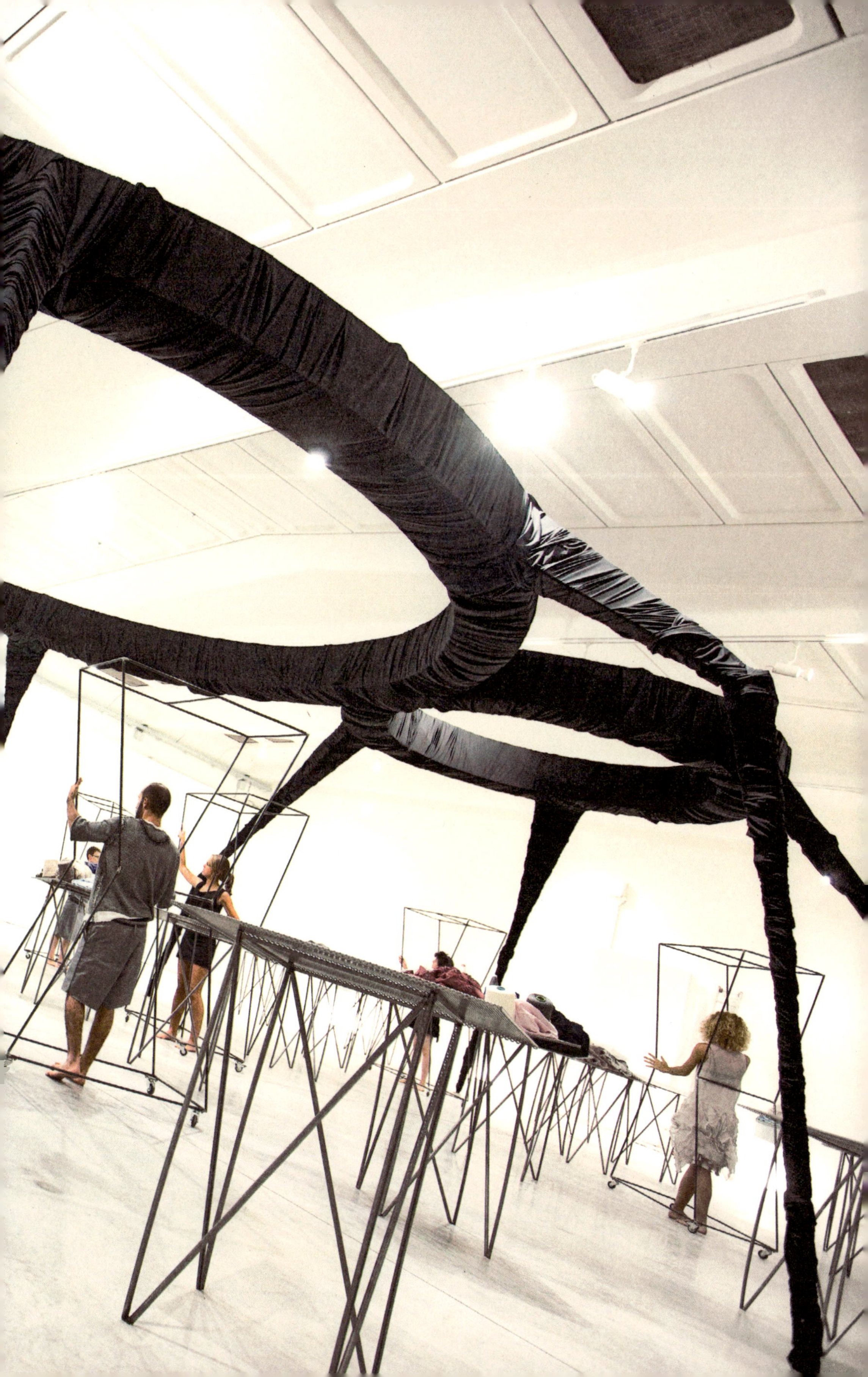

# Democracy as the balancing of differences

In my work the recognition of differences commenced with the first mirror picture in 1961. I will try, in this connection, to explain how they work. The picture is made up of two elements: the mirror that shows images in their incessant movement, and the photographic figure fixed onto the mirror, which remains motionless forever. In this way total mobility and the maximum of immobility are obtained at one and the same time: two realities–one the opposite of the other–that coexist in the same place. These extreme differences meet and are perfectly united in the mirror picture, recalling in this convergence all the opposing dualities: dynamic and static, unity and multiplicity, front and back, near and far, presence and absence, surface and depth, absolute and relative, tangible and intangible. All comprised in the relationship between positive and negative. Polarization of all the different signs occurs in the mirror picture.

We know that the right connection between a positive and a negative pole generates energy for our civilization, like the power that lights the bulb. On the other hand the electrical energy that manifests itself freely in nature can have devastating effects, as in the case of the lightning bolt that burns down forests or houses. In society, when differences are not joined in a fruitful way, pernicious conflicts are inevitably generated. If not carefully joined, in fact, opposite polarities constitute a continual threat to civilized coexistence. Thus too, in the moral sense, the more the very concepts of good and evil are dismissed, the greater is the possibility of exacerbating conflict, creating the bolts of lightning that strike society and spark off wars. In the symbol of the

Third Paradise this polarization is represented by the central circle that is charged with the energy of the two lateral circles, the natural and the artificial.

In the Third Paradise a balance between the various aspects of social life and between the most conflicting moral conceptions is made possible. In it a civilization is shaped in which differences are not driven apart, but brought together to produce convergence, coexistence, understanding, sharing and exchange.

To make what I am saying clear, I think it is necessary to clarify the concept of symbol itself. Its etymological root is the Greek *symbolon*, a term that indicates two sections of a divided unit which, even when they are pushed apart, always tend toward a reunification. The symbol is a pact that can be used to avoid or resolve a possible conflict between the parts. Hence the symbol of the Third Paradise is a call for the bringing together of two realities that over time have become antagonistic: nature and artifice. Its function is to draw the parts toward an accord.

I created the Third Paradise because I sensed that the world needed to be able to identify with a symbol that would indicate the solution to conflicts that have reached a level of global unsustainability. After coming up with the symbol, I set about translating its meaning into reality, involving society directly. It is obvious that my creative efforts can only be addressed both to the symbol and to its reification in the practical sense. For this reason, it is evident that the process of action of the Third Paradise affects the whole sphere of human life, thereby taking on an almost mythical value. I have been told that the commitment to transforming society, as it is understood in the Third Paradise, appears to be a mythical enterprise.

Mythology is filled with tales of extraordinary feats carried out by heroes or gods, through which humanity seeks to give meaning to its existence. Heroism entails uncommon deeds that often lead to sacrifice. This is the case with Osiris, Baal, Dionysus, Adonis and Attis–condensed in the figure of Jesus himself–who face death and pass through it as an extreme test of truth. All these figures performed great exploits and found their consecration through sacrifice.

Even on the news we come across similar phenomena. Michael Jackson, for example, one of the best-known performers in the world of music in the eighties before falling out of favor, became a myth only with his death, the conclusion of the aesthetic and psychological torture he had inflicted on himself. The Third Paradise distances itself, however, from any sense of sacrifice, as it has been formed out of a desire for life rather than death, and does not stem from the heroism of a champion, but from collective awareness: in human and earthly, not transcendent conditions. It does not require individuals to adhere to a truth established through the tragic act of a person. In this new concept of myth we are thinking, therefore, not of the verticality of a higher oneness but of the horizontality that recognizes and embraces differences.

The political bureau of Cittadellarte has launched Love Difference–a Mediterranean Cultural Network. The aim of this artistic movement is to link up people and institutions in the regions bordering the Mediterranean Sea that are interested in creating new perspectives which can lead beyond the tragic conflict between different cultures and societies. Love Difference is, therefore, a programmatic presage that, through art's capacity to be a common root of all humanity, it is possible to reconcile transnational differences. The movement focuses its activity on the Mediterranean area, which links three continents in which the problems of global society are mirrored.

A policy that leads people to "love differences" is vital to the development of new prospects in the whole body of society. The name of the movement, Love Difference, surpasses the concept of "tolerance" of diversity–which reflects a rational forbearance–and penetrates directly into the realm of feeling: "loving" means "feeling attraction, emotion," "expressing affection and devotion." The differences between people and social groups are the first thing to be embraced in an open, sensitive and warm way if we want to finally give meaning to the word "humanity." A new thinking has to underpin economics and politics and the place in which it is forged could be the creative workshop of a socially engaged art. Love Difference–a movement of ideas–was born in this workshop. Political systems, in the traditional sense, are now displaying insufficient ability to tackle and solve the great problems inherent in the cultural transformation underway that concerns world society and the physical state of the planet. Art, a primary expression of creativity, assumes a social responsibility, playing an active part in the construction of a new civilization on a worldwide scale. The Love Difference movement has focused on the countries that surround the Mediterranean Sea, but at the same time extends its activity, as far as possible, to other seas in the world that can be seen as "mediterranean": the great basins surrounded by land that have given rise to different cultures, traditions, economies and ancient and modern political systems. So this project includes the Red Sea, the Black Sea, the South China Sea, the Sea of Japan, the Baltic Sea and the Caribbean Sea.

In June 2008 Love Difference made an important commitment to the formation of a network of connections between the different countries that, along with Italy, surround the Mediterranean Sea proper. On that date in fact the Mediterranean Cultural Parliament was set up. In its founding charter we find the following: "[...] Our mobilization reflects an impelling need to act. The creation of a Mediterranean Cultural Parliament expresses our determination to establish a space for meetings that can also serve as an instrument of common actions. To this end, the Mediterranean Cultural Parliament brings together the free and responsible individuals who are present in every region to work together both on small-scale actions and on far-ranging programs. The Parliament proposes, to all those who wish to join it, a plan of flexible, autonomous and open interventions, with the aim of favoring the interaction of common experiences, germinating initiatives and producing and sharing works."

In this way art assumes the formative value of a new sociopolitical ethics, providing valid models and examples to imitate. More than words, it is modes of behavior and actions that result in the correct functioning of civil life. If I recommend something to my children but do the exact opposite, they will take on board what I do, forgetting my words. Sometimes parents, acting differently from what they say, use the threat of punishment to get their children to obey their commands, creating a schizophrenic situation that affects their mental balance. Rules are derived from human action and propose an idea of common good. Ethics, if framed in commandments and laws like those put forward by religions, remains bound to dictates that are to a large extent expressed as prohibitions. For practical reasons, people are made to respect these by inculcating a fear of divine retribution or punishment. And so the individual, instead of basing his or her actions on a rational acceptance of the rules, obeys them out of fear of the consequences.

In this way the rational part of the persona is not developed, but the emotional side is radicalized. It seems to me, therefore, that before all else it is necessary to work on increasing people's capacity to balance emotion with reason. Science has introduced the method by which a law, for instance that of thermodynamics, corresponds to a verifiable result. The Third Paradise takes a prudent approach to the human that does not overstep the limits of the scientific method. It fosters a direct responsibility of the individual person, which affects the community in turn, shaping an idea of justice that involves, in idea and in practice, the life of the polis, presupposing a democratic sharing of knowledge. If laws are broken by the lawmakers–as unfortunately history has shown to be the case up to now– the same schizophrenic situation is created in society as we described earlier in a certain type of relationship between parents and children.

We must, in short, become aware of ourselves as individuals who belong to a society that is at once local and global. The 20th century has been a political experiment in which an attempt was made to understand which counted more, the individual or the group, through the opposition between the extremes of capitalism and communism. This question has still not been resolved today and grave situations of social schizophrenia persist, fueling, as we see every day, national and international conflict. There is a collective consciousness that has to be analyzed and freed from the vices that in the past have crystallized in society through the forms of education. This result can be attained with a twofold action: on the one hand aimed at developing awareness and knowledge of oneself, on the other at fostering the same qualities in the social sphere. I believe it is necessary to carry out a psychoanalysis of society in the same way as is done for the individual: we need to diagnose the human community to find out what is wrong and to cure it. Freud identified traumas that had their roots in the patient's childhood, but we have to consider that society itself suffers from problems that emerged at its origins and have grown worse as it developed. Societies have been nursed, raised and educated by religious and political systems that have shaped its characteristics. This education leaves us not just with psychological defects but also with physical problems that stem from modern consumerist culture. While we must acknowledge the extraordinary achievements of medical science in its extension of our lifespan, there are still vast areas of the world that live in conditions of absolute poverty and cannot benefit from medical advances. Where, on the other hand, the consumer system has incorporated the sphere of medicine as well, the individual is induced to delegate his or her health, creating a sense of passivity and lack of responsibility.

Today we tend to neglect the biological knowledge of our body, failing to take the preventive measures that we could instead apply on a daily basis. The more individuals ignore their bodies, the more they will rely on, in addition to the treatments prescribed, the irresponsible consumption of medicine, encouraged by the advertising industry. This chain makes clear the need for self-control, at the physical level too, putting us in a condition of avoid the emergence of disorders through the development of a greater empathy with the biology of our organism. Health is indissolubly bound up with the daily lives we lead and with the way we nourish the body; every conscious or unconscious choice we make eventually affects our wellbeing.

Let us look at some moments of the day and the effects they have on us. The choice of the ingredients in our cooking entails the possibility of opting for animal or vegetable products. The decision to eat meat, milk, eggs or cheese leads to an increase in the amount of land given over to intensive farming–whether on the ground, in cages or free range–as well as that used for the production of fodder, organic or not. Should we choose vegetables and cereals we are faced with the problem of the seasonal character of crops and of the presence of pesticides and artificial fertilizers. Both choices influence the economic and environmental structure of the world. Finally, we will have to decide whether to place on our table jugs filled with water from the faucet or mineral water bought at the store or supermarket, packaged in glass or plastic bottles; whether to drink wine, beer or beverages that are chemically altered during the process of their production.

Among the causes of illness today we are seeing an exponential increase in the stress generated by lifestyles too distant from the ones that are natural for human beings. Reduced physical activity and the psychological stress that results from the acceleration of work pace and

the lack of daily contact with nature, combined with an unbalanced and excessive diet, are some of the principal causes of heart attacks and cancers in the industrialized countries. In the last analysis even social aspects–the world of relationships, with friends, colleagues and the family–can give rise to illness, depression or nervous breakdown. If we look at the rise in drug taking, we will find at the sociological level that inadequacy in relationship, the difficulty we have in handling social intercourse in an active and constructive manner and in accepting ourselves for what we are, are among the prime factors of dependence on so-called "artificial paradises." The illusory compensatory effect that drugs can provide at the expense of the user's health needs to be seen in the light of the responsible acts that bring balance to society; from consumers of "paradises" we have to become producers of a real and everyday paradise.
I believe that it has been made clear in these few lines that the question of health is a profoundly political one and has to tackled with extreme care. The "health" of a population can be judged from its political capacity to intervene in the environment to favor, especially in the weakest and most "vulnerable," the ability of people to acquire faith in themselves and as a consequence to foster that physical and mental harmony of which both the individual and society are in dire need. On this harmony is founded the change of tack required to achieve a real political transformation of society. A healthy individual in a healthy society: this ought to be written in the first article of every constitution.

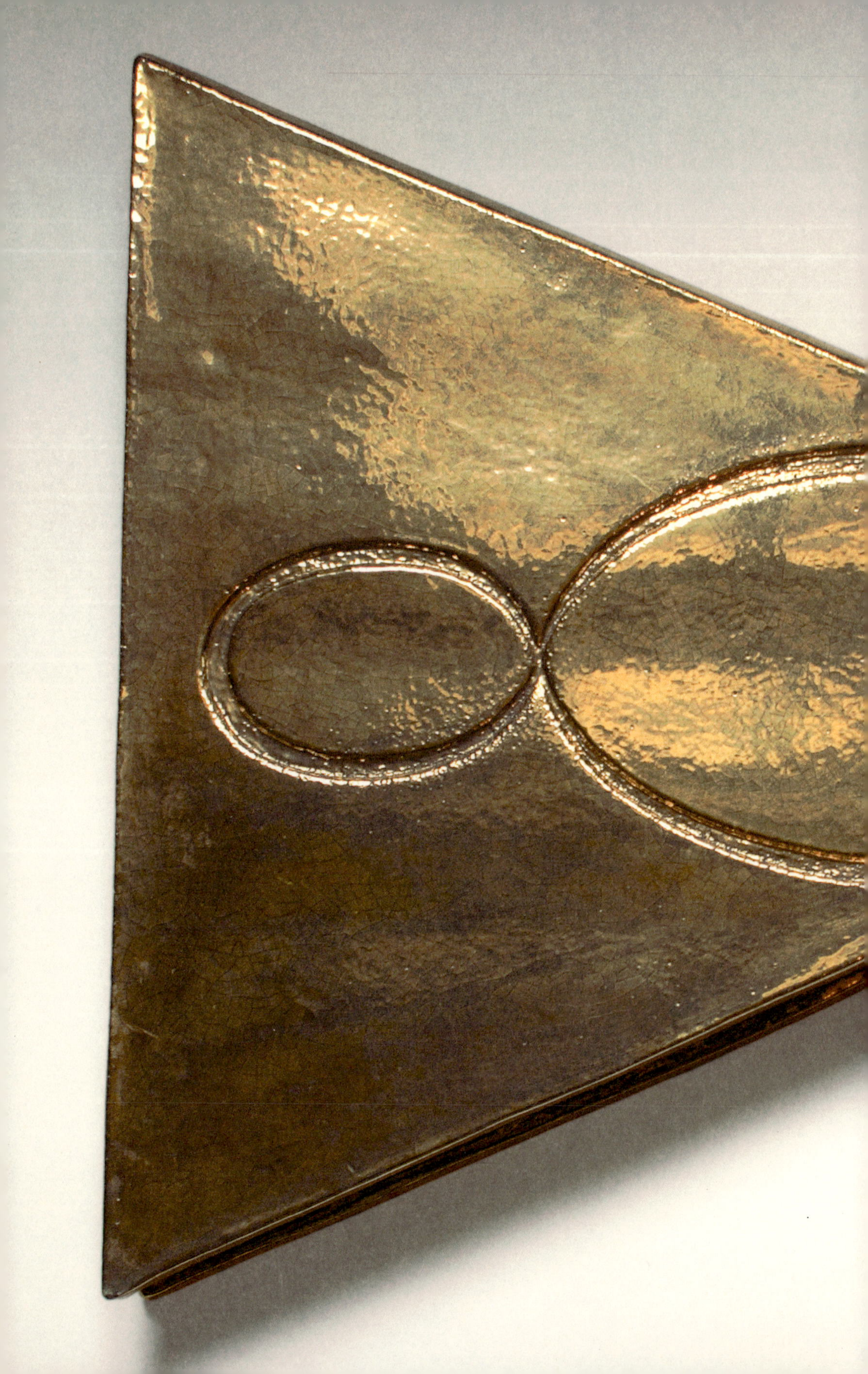

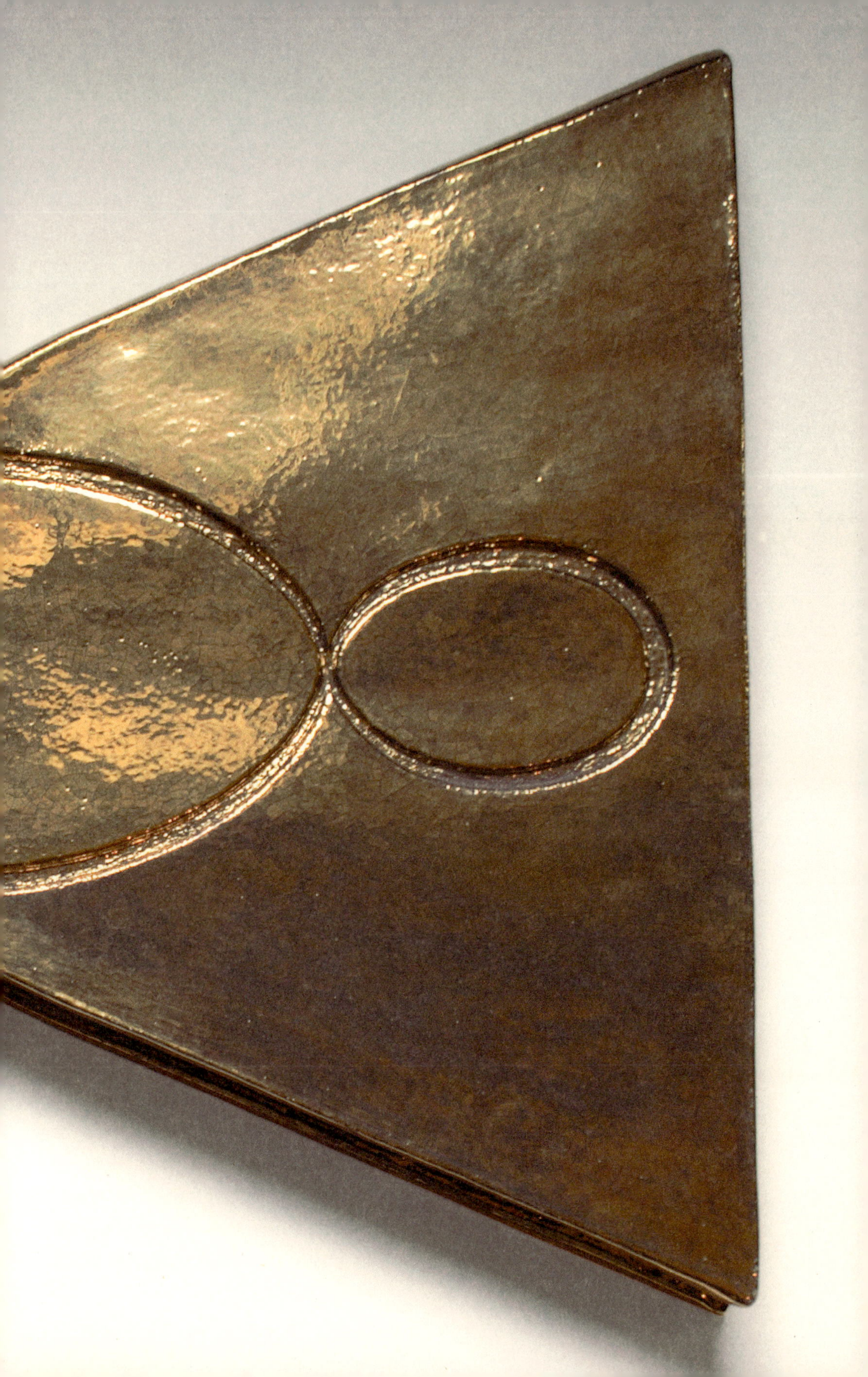

# Freedom as generator of responsibility

The "second paradise" was born out of human creativity. Up to now we have been unable to define what creativity is from a scientific perspective; we can simply ascertain that it exists. It is perhaps what distinguishes humans from animals and from every other form of life, or at least what differentiates them in the quantity and quality with which it manifests itself. Most modern naturalists claim that it is impossible to regard human abilities as wholly detached and distant from those of animals, contradicting the theories that hold humanity to be an exception in the biological world, created out of nothing by divine will.

Personally, I go along with the theories that do not separate the anthroposphere, the world of human beings, from the theriosphere, the world of animals. It cannot, in fact, be said that creativity appeared out of the blue, while it is conceivable that it developed through a process linked to the evolution of the human brain as it passed from a primitive state, similar to that of our closest relative among species (the chimpanzees that had already begun to use tools), to a progressive improvement of those tools.

What do we mean by tool? It is the conscious interposition of an object–be it a club or a computer–between oneself and the other to attain a precise end. By testing the consequences of using tools human beings broadened their possibilities of understanding: perceiving the phenomenon of cause and effect produced an association of ideas. In this way they advanced by exploring and exploiting causal relationships. The hand that, in the Paleolithic, deliberately left its imprint on the wall of a cave transformed its physicality into representation.

This imprint is a mirror of intelligence. In this way two primary elements can be identified: one is the practical tool, the other is the tool of idea and representation. Intellectual development occurs in parallel with technical development: the mark intentionally left by the hand on the rock can be considered the first work of art in history and thus also identified as the decisive transition from the animal state to the human one. From this point on humanity passed through successive phases of refinement with regard both to tools and the image, the imagination and its transposition into symbols. While humans chipped flints for hunting, they painted animals and scenes of their capture in caves. And science, heir to the primitive tool-making part of the human intelligence, advanced jointly with ideal and representative thought.

*previous pages*
*Golden Book*
*of the Third Paradise,*
ceramics, 2006
photo: Juan Esteban Sandoval

It might seem, from what has been said, that the development of tools and technology and intellectual development have together followed a perfectly harmonious and peaceful course. Yet there is a conflict between them, whose causes should be sought in the very nature of the "tool," which bears within it the animal principles of offense to obtain food and defense against external threats. This conflict is not solely with the outside environment, but also takes place within our own species, human against human: an animal system of predation has been reconstituted in the human race. What I am trying to say is that within humankind groups have formed–as if they were different races–and each group-race has seen the others as animals to be preyed on, attacked, exploited and robbed of their material and immaterial possessions. The phenomenon has not disappeared over the course of time, but has continued throughout history, with terrifying examples right up to the present day. It suffices to think of European colonization, during which indigenous populations were regarded, treated and used exactly as if they were animals, or of the extermination to which not just Jews but other ethnic groups and categories of human beings were subjected under Nazism, when the killing of people was justified on the grounds that they were considered no more than animals. This shows how the speculation of the mind can arrive at a totally arbitrary and distorted vision of reality and how such alienation can infect entire communities. We have to admit, consequently, that human creativity does not find expression solely in constructive

intelligence, but can also have devastating destructive effects. In the 20th century art gradually assumed an independence and an attitude of critical judgment with regard to what was going on in the world. Before and after the Second World War we can find significant examples of works denouncing the atrocities of which we have spoken. They include Pablo Picasso's *Guernica* (which explores the madness of a moment in history), Primo Levi's *Se questo è un uomo* (published in America as *Survival in Auschwitz*, the autobiographical account of his experience in Nazi concentration camps) and Luigi Nono's *Il canto sospeso*, *Ricorda cosa ti hanno fatto in Auschwitz* and *La victoire de Guernica*. We ourselves, at this point in history and starting out from forms of denunciation like these, have to recognize the responsibility that creativity has had in developing human intelligence, draw our conclusions and set a new process in motion. Humanity finds itself in front of a true mirror that reflects the whole of the journey it has made. In 15th-century Florence artists and architects worked out the perspective that has led us to the reality of modern life, where it has found its fulfillment. At the age of eighteen–a time when I was looking for directions to take in my work as an artist–I had the opportunity to see Piero della Francesca's *Flagellation* in Urbino, a work that played a fundamental part in the definition of Renaissance perspective. In this painting the structure of the perspective determines the composition of the picture absolutely; the religious subject of the work is a mere pretext. There is none of the dramatic expressiveness suggested by the theme of Christ's scourging and the figures located in the different parts of the picture appear to be no more than geometric references for the phenomenon of perspective.
The work immediately gave me the idea for something that has come a primary commitment for me: starting out from modernity and discovering with art a new perspective for society, just as the Renaissance had done with respect to the Middle Ages. Research led me to the mirror picture. An unlimited perspective vision opens in the mirror, but one that, in its reflection, shows us everything that is behind us and obliges us to consider the space and time that extends at our back. This is the mirror in front of which we find ourselves today. It has to be said that in this rearview perspective humanity sees itself in the mirror, as if examining everything it has done.

Looking in this mirror we have to find the capacity to resolve the conflict between the extraordinary advance of scientific progress and its cultural utilization, still constrained and limited by hoary beliefs and outdated and unresolved forms of relationship. This is made possible by a new conception of the human that will allow us to break the vicious circle still expressed aptly today by the Latin phrase *homo homini lupus*, or "man is a wolf to [his fellow] man."

Science has reached the heights it has today precisely because it is founded on the assumption that every aspect of reality is determined by phenomenological relations. Today we are able to conceive these relations rationally without following an impulsive instinct, without abandoning ourselves to the consolations offered by systems based on faith. In saying this it is not my intention to play down the importance of the feelings with respect to reason, but their function has to be understood in terms of the relationship between cause and effect.

This is why it is necessary to find an understanding between art and science, making ever more productive the combination of freedom, sensitivity, emotion, the responsibility for verification and the exercise of reason that in various ways the two disciplines share.

For an important textile manufacturer in the Biella region I came up with the slogan "the hand–the mind–the product–the environment," reflecting the awareness that a complex set of cultural as well as technical elements are involved in the manufacturing system too. The hand and mind are coordinated in one of the oldest expressions of human industriousness and the environment today is dependent on the choices made by systems of production. The ability to create refined fabrics ought to be applied to the fabric of society as well, in a harmonious combination of both aspects: the scientific and technical one and the artistic and cultural one. If we look at the technique of weaving, moreover, the two different spheres can be compared to the warp and the weft, a binary system that, curiously, is also the basis of calculation with the computer.

The ability to integrate art and science with the various sectors of the social structure, such as manufacturing, economics, politics, education and communication, heralds a new classicism. A classicism no longer understood as a phenomenon exclusive to Western culture, but as a practice of balance and proportion shared by the entire human

fig. 1
The navel is the crucial point through which pass the lines that separate and at the same time link in mirror symmetry the top and the bottom, the left and the right of the human body. The navel always remains the central point and gives rise to the "umbilical cross."

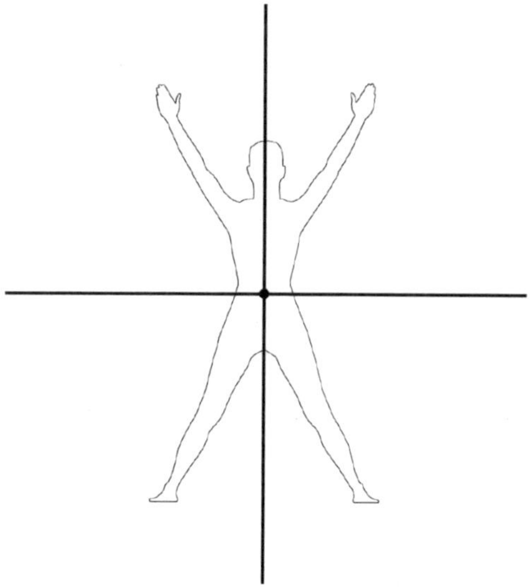

fig. 2
Viewed from the front the trunk of the body human occupies a fixed part, while legs and arms are mobile. I spread the legs to form an equilateral triangle and for symmetry I open the arms, creating another equilateral triangle. In this way I obtain two triangles that are mirror images.

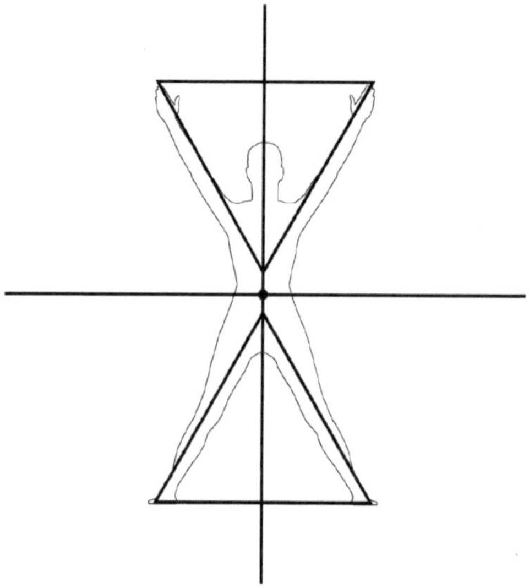

fig. 3
I trace a circumference around the body human that touches the ends of the outspread legs and arms.

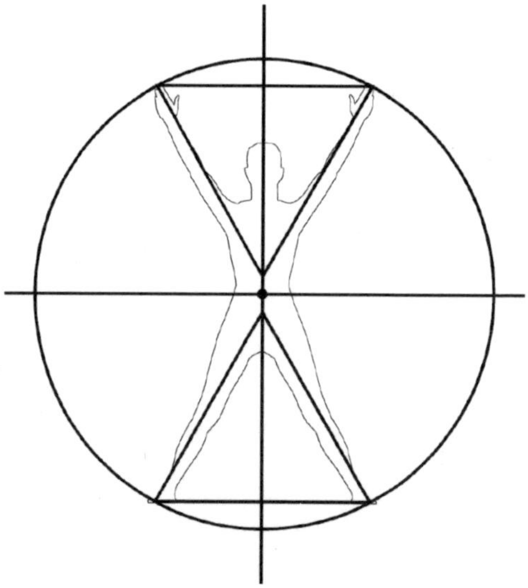

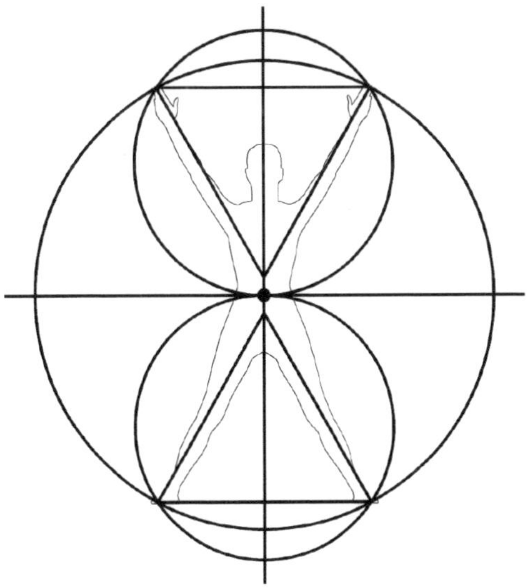

fig. 4
I draw two circumferences, one touching the navel and the hands, the other the navel and the feet, that intersect the larger circumference.

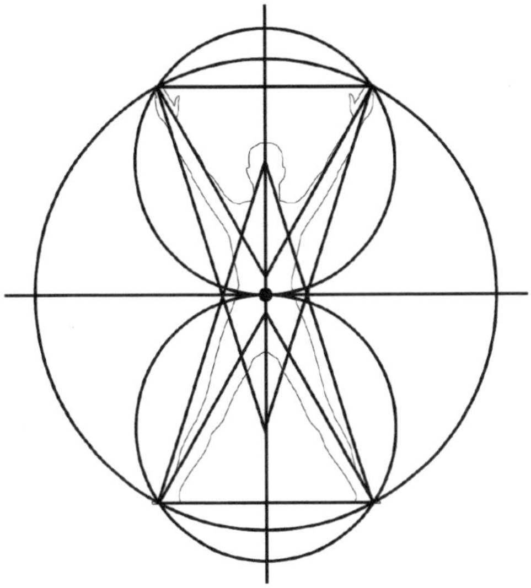

fig. 5
From the center of the upper circumference I trace two lines that meet the lower circumference at the feet, forming an isosceles triangle. The same isosceles triangle is formed by inverting the operation and tracing two lines from the center of the lower circumference that meet the upper circumference at the points where it touches the hands.

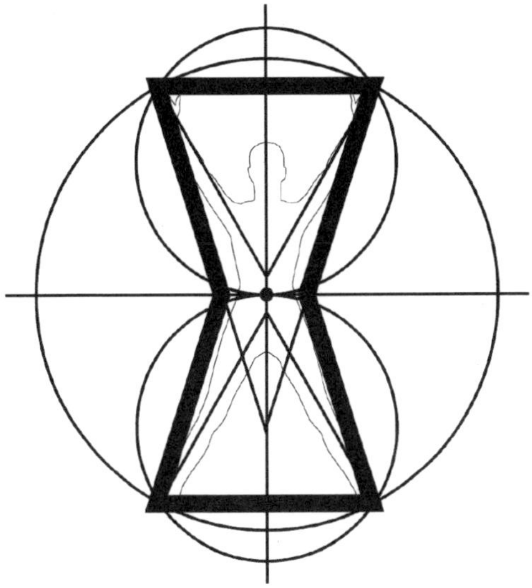

fig. 6
I emphasize the perimeter of the polygon created by the intersection of the two isosceles triangles, a meeting that occurs on the horizontal axis–often called the "life line"–of the umbilical cross. In this way I obtain the *Art Sign*.

race. With this in mind I traced on the mirror a sign that schematized a new equilibrium of the geometric proportions of the body human: with them I established an organic relationship between the person and the reality of which he or she is part.

Leon Battista Alberti–the architect who along with Piero della Francesca developed the science of perspective–declared that he was aiming at the sum total of knowledge through the mathematical reconstruction of the world. This same intention lies behind Leonardo's famous drawing–linked with his studies of Vitruvius–that inscribes the human figure in both a circle and a square. Recently this drawing has appeared in numerous publications and this goes to show that the need is felt for a new renaissance. In my view, however, the use of Leonardo's study runs the risk of remaining specious and redundant if its meaning is not updated so that it answers to the requirements of the present day. In Leonardo's drawing the human figure is adapted to geometric forms. The sign I traced on the mirror–which I called *Segno Arte* or *Art Sign*–reveals instead a geometric structure that is defined on the basis of the human body. For the sake of clarity I will explain the genesis of this sign with the aid of images.

*following pages*
Pistoletto
and Cittadellarte
*The Third Paradise,*
La Spezia, CAMeC, 2007
photo: Enrico Amici

It is these geometric proportions of the human figure that formed the basis for my reasoning about a real quest for balance, extended onto the plane of society. In the first place I replaced the male figure with a female one, underlining the central role of the procreating womb. In the *Art Sign* it is precisely the woman's navel that becomes an emblem of the fourth dimension, *time*. The umbilical cord is the means used to feed the fetus during the intrauterine phase and its cutting at birth impresses a mark at the center of the person that links her with the past and future of humanity. Through our umbilical cords we go back, in fact, to the past, arriving at the first placental mammals, and project ourselves into the future through the generations to come. The *Art Sign* is first of all a symbol of life and can be superimposed on that of the Third Paradise, whose central circle is conceived as a womb that contains the next generations. In its greatest extension the *Art Sign*, which incorporates the human figure, is emblematic of the perfect equilibrium. Centered as it is on the "umbilical cross," it becomes essentially a symbol of life. I have created a physical version of the *Art Sign*, giving it the function of a door through which a person can actually pass. Anyone who passes through the *Art Sign Door* makes, metaphorically, his or her entrance into society.

The prehistoric imprint of the hand on the wall of the cave is for me the first "Art Sign" in history, which with today's *Art Sign* achieves the completeness of the whole body. Leonardo's man was placed at the center of a world still to be discovered. Today, the *Art Sign* made from a mirror configures a human being who projects herself into the future by looking into the past, like a temporal balance, and directs the attention toward new proportions that humanity has to consider in order to go further.

If we look at the socioeconomic statistics, however, we can see just how far we are from those proportions. From them, in fact, we get an image of global society that can be represented as a deformed body made up of two triangles, a little one at the top, by way of a head, in which wealth and power are concentrated, and another that broadens progressively towards the bottom, where poverty and degradation are rife. Clearly the economy is symptomatic of all the dysfunctions from which humanity suffers. For me, trying to make this social figure proportionate, by bringing it to the equilibrium defined by the *Art Sign*, is an artistic task worth devoting myself to completely. I speak and act as an artist, taking advantage of the freedom that art acquired in the 20th century and knowing well that such freedom brings with it an equal responsibility: the freer you are the more responsible you are. Everyone should assume the measure of freedom that allows them to manifest most responsibility; fortunately there are already energetic people who devote their freedom to practices of social utility, forming groups, associations and institutions capable of working together for a *responsible social transformation*. The slowness of the major political systems in finding a remedy for the worldwide emergency is truly worrying. So it is of decisive importance that the agents already at work on change should multiply in order to make participation in the common project of giving a new form to society increasingly pervasive.

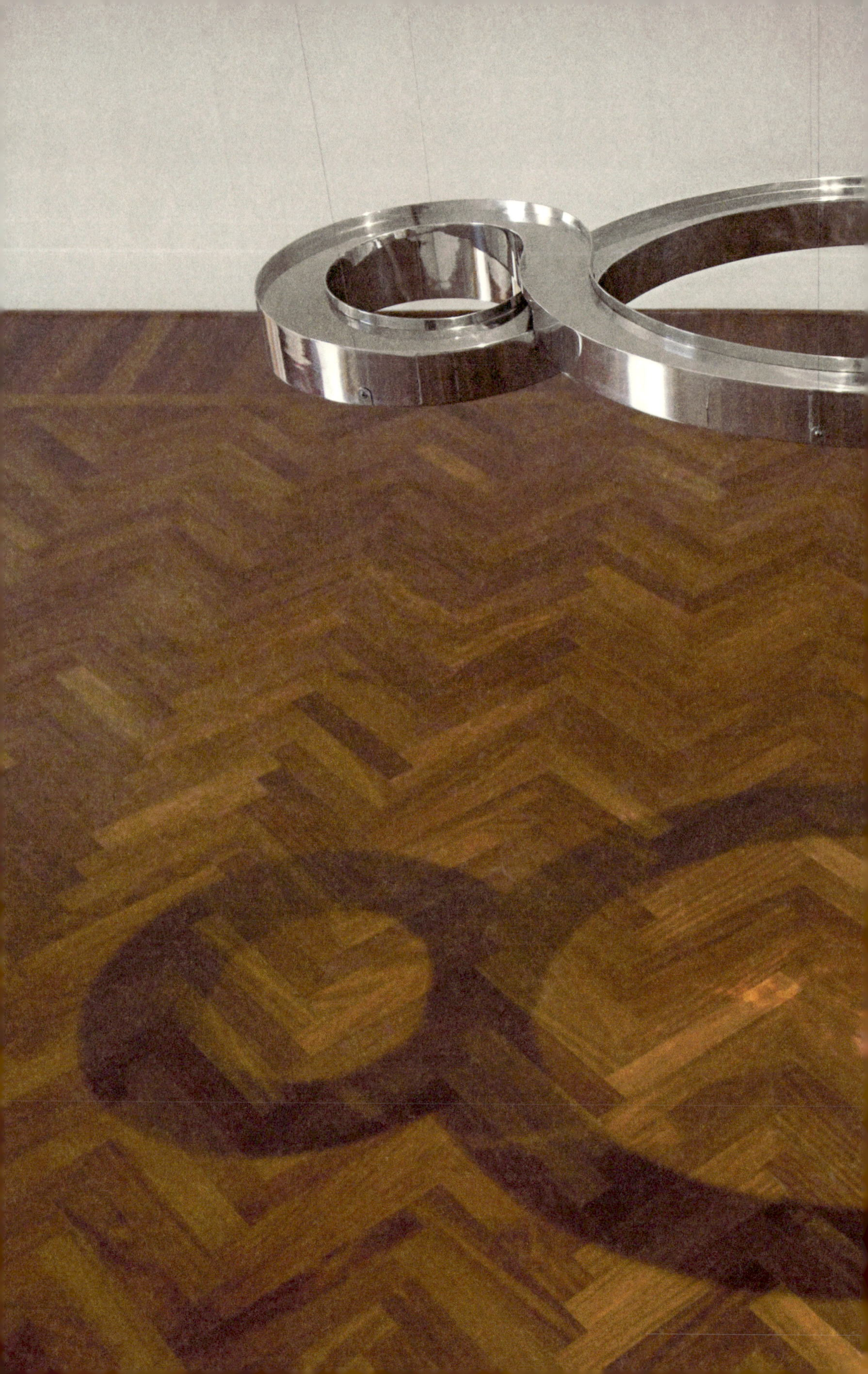

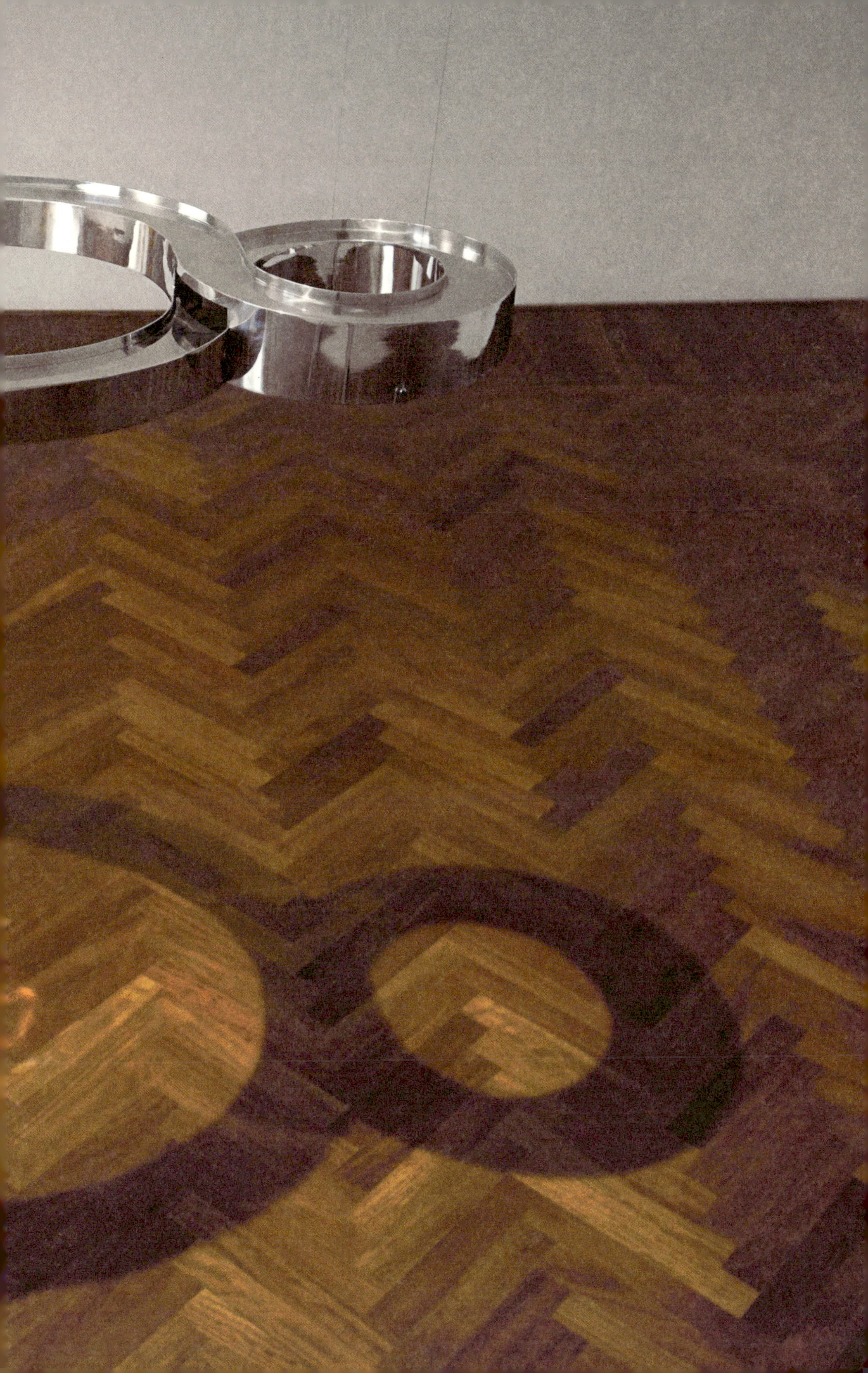

# Art as spirituality

Ever since the origins the representation of images has had a magical and apotropaic character. At the time when our ancestors were chipping flints to make arrowheads in their caves, they drew their prey and scenes of their capture on the walls to propitiate the spirit of the hunt. With these paintings art became a sign of spirituality, becoming the starting point for religion and its social content. It was already a ritual practice that inevitably drew its substance from magic.

How can the emergence of the magical component in human thought be explained? James Frazer wrote: "I am coming more and more to the conclusion that if we define religion as the attempt to propitiate natural and supernatural powers, and magic as a coercion exercised on them, then magic has always preceded religion. When men realize, on the basis of their experience, that they are unable to compel higher powers to satisfy their desires, only then do they resign themselves to imploring them. With the passing of time, then, they begin to grasp that supplication is also vain, and therefore try with coercion again; but this time the coercion is applied within narrower limits, and in a different way from the old magical method. In short, religion is replaced by science. The order of evolution, then, of human thought and practice is magic–religion–science. Currently, we are living in an era of transition between religion and science, an era that will last, of course, for many generations to come. It is up to those who have progress at heart to do what they can to aid the eventual triumph of science in their time."

In the impossibility of obtaining scientific evidence, therefore, humanity has always come up with mystical answers that lie outside the logical and objective dimension and that continue to carry weight in the age of science. The space between the magical and the mystical is occupied by that third term which we call spirituality and which has become the terrain on which the religions have founded their dogmas. "Spirituality" and "religion" are still generally, but improperly, used as synonyms, but there are expressions of spirituality even in nonbelievers. I think, in any case, that artistic inspiration is directly connected with the concept of spirituality, as is evident from their common etymological root *spiritus* or "breath," with the verb "to inspire" signifying "to breathe in," "to instill a thought in the mind." For this reason art has had an empathetic relationship with myths and religions. In the history of the West the artist used to invoke the muses to obtain inspiration, just as the primitive hunter invoked the spirit of the hunt. From the Renaissance onward, however, the artist became his own muse, introducing his independence even into the sacred subject. With the mathematically determined perspective of the Renaissance a vision was created that distanced the magical element from the representation of reality. Then the practice of psychological investigation of the human being was introduced: no longer an anonymous human being, like the creators of Christian icons from Byzantium to the Middle Ages, but protagonist of his own sign, summing up all his responsibility in his signature. Nevertheless, up until the 19th century, the originality of the artist still found expression within his function of serving the needs of his religious, political or civil clients.

From the end of the 19th century, following the industrial revolution, the artist–whether painter or sculptor–also freed himself from representation and from all previous forms of service. Having to deal with the advent of photography, the artist was obliged to move away from any function that this was able to perform automatically. Nothing was left for art but to carry out a "self-analysis," exploring all of its possibilities. In this research the visual artist reached the point in which he found himself alone with his own sign and, as if bringing his hand back to its imprint, eliminated all the interpositions laid down in the past. It was a starting over *ab ovo* that became emblematic with Piero Manzoni's fingerprint on an egg. This work sums up the historical phase that the avant-garde went through in the fifties, characterized by nonrepresentational art and abstract expressionism. In this way the individual sign of each artist took the place of the universal symbols with which art had coexisted up until then, including them all in the subjectivity of the artist himself. The sense of spirituality contained in the works of the past was shared by entire peoples, whereas it now became the responsibility of the artist, who concentrated it in his own sign, substituting it for any other symbology. The spirituality of art disengaged itself totally from the symbols that came from the past, squeezed instead into the persona of the artist alone and withering its existential foundations. The fact of having concentrated on themselves the whole history of human thought, obviously, produced in some artists an almost unbearable compression that led them more or less directly to suicide. I myself experienced in the fifties the state of solitude stemming from this condition. If the avant-garde tendencies had eliminated any sign apart from the individual one, I reacted to this in my research by eliminating even the individual sign in which the whole weight of the human tragedy had been condensed. With my art, in fact, I had to take myself out of that tragedy. The work was transformed from subjective to objective through the replacement of the canvas of the picture by a mirror. It is not just my sign, my hand or my personality that is impressed on the mirror picture, but everything that there is in the physical universe impacts on the surface of the mirror and is replicated within it. In front of and inside the mirror everything that that can exist expands infinitely. Eliminating any sign, including my own, I brought back to the world the art that had been taken away from it.

In 2000 I created, at the Paoli-Calmettes cancer hospital in Marseilles, a multi-confessional place of meditation and prayer in which the symbols of the major religions and a secular space surround one of my works from 1966 entitled *Cubic Meter of Infinity*. This is a parallelepiped composed of six mirrors facing inward: we only see the back of the mirrors that make up the cube, while inside the mirrors reflect themselves endlessly. In this work the infinite can be perceived only by the mind and it excludes the tangibility of the senses. Yet the imagination enters the cube and expands in a boundless dimension, comprehending the process that has generated it as well. Through this "self-reflecting cubic meter" we reach the point of contact between the infinite and the finite. The intangible infinity contained in the cube loses a degree of its intangibility because it is produced in a tangible body, so this work is *infinity minus one*. So we can also say that everything in existence, subtracting itself from the infinite, is infinity minus one. The fact that I am able to make my thought reach the point in which infinity and one touch each other means that I'm projecting my intelligence into a universal dimension: and if it is possible to enter this dimension with thought, then it can be said that infinity is a universal intelligence minus one, my own. Everything that exists is part of the same intelligence. When all is said and done human beings are not separate from nature, but they have removed themselves from it just far enough to become a mirror of natural intelligence.

Ever since the fifties I have felt the need to take the autonomy of art–gradually acquired over the course of the first half of the 20th century–in the direction of a shared and plural universal perspective. In the design of the place of meditation that replaced the earlier Catholic chapel in the hospital in Marseilles it was not my intention to make the independence of art an exclusive concept, but I did set art at the center of a transformation of thinking that would involve people belonging to different religions and even those who do not identify with any of them.

Religions play a decisive role in shaping the individual identity and community customs. The different phases of social life have been punctuated by *ritual forms of passage* since the most remote times and at every latitude. Art cannot disregard the need to give a socially symbolic value to significant moments in human life, so it has to develop forms that can introduce, into rituality, an ever more autonomous awareness on the part of people. This does not mean leaving individuals alone with themselves, but offering them references that can be shared, capable of freeing them from the mesh of a collective moral subjugation.

In all this the existential need to tackle the relationship between known and unknown, person and universe, remains urgent. In different times and places people have turned to the transcendent to find an answer to these questions: for example, the polytheistic deities acted as a link between the human and the superhuman, while the monotheistic faiths have conceived a single creator god, outside the universe. If this god has created what exists, then what exists is the work of god. In the same way we say that a work of art is the artist's work, for we are accustomed to seeing the artist as separate from his work. With the *mirror picture* I entered directly into the work and brought the whole world with me. Following this experience I acted in the awareness of being myself part of the work. With this awareness I embarked on an exploration of performance in which, in my own physicality, I was the work. With the group called The Zoo at the end of the sixties, I set in motion a creative participation between artists coming from the most diverse fields, in which each one acted at one and the same time as author of himself and of the group. Extending the reasoning to a universal level, we can make creator and work coincide. Just as in a broken mirror each fragment possesses the same qualities as the whole mirror, each individual has the same properties as the universe. In this connection it may be illuminating to refer to another of my works that I created in 1973, entitled *Self-Portrait of Stars*. In it the photographic silhouette of my body appears on a large sheet of transparent film, life size and containing a vast slice of the sky filled with galaxies photographed from an astronomical observatory. The effect of the interpenetration between the two images is striking. On the small scale of my figure it is possible to recognize an immense portion of the universe, and that immense portion of the universe can be recognized through the small dimensions of my figure. What we see is a human body expanded to the cosmic scale and at the same time the cosmos concentrated in a human body. Obviously the work could have used the image of an animal or an object, but it is the human being who seeks answers to questions on existence.

A further reflection, in this connection, leads us to the subject of life and death. In the mirror we can see that every event in the present is always different from the one that precedes it and from the one that follows it: so every instant that appears in it is born and dies simultaneously. It suffices to stop in front of a mirror to note that in it each image exists just for a moment: before it was not there and after it is no longer there. The present can be understood as the length of each life reduced to an instant. In physical reality, on the other hand, the passage between life and death is prolonged in different forms, dimensions and periods. The traditional mathematical symbol for infinity, traced with an unbroken line, can represent great movements in time and space. The point at which the line intersects itself, creating two circles, is the present that transforms everything that has been realized in the previous curve into what will be realized in the following curve, just as a person who dies comes back to life with a different form. The symbol of the Third Paradise, as has already been pointed out, utilizes the mathematical symbol for infinity but forms a third circle at the line's point of intersection. In it extends the organic space of each person in his or her life on Earth.

In the womb of the Third Paradise a spirituality can be developed in conjunction with a truly enlightened art, in so far as the human being arrives at an awareness of being a thinking and acting part of the universe. In this way we come to a conception of immanent rather than transcendent spirituality. And it is precisely on the immanent conception of the Third Paradise that I would like to dwell. Someone once asked me if, in this case, I was not putting my signature on an age just as I had previously signed a year, with the work *White Year*. To answer this it will be helpful to illustrate this work briefly.

Since 1985 I had been creating dark and gloomy works, lumped together under the title the *Art of Squalor*. In December 1988, invited to show some of these works in the spaces of Opera at Perugia, I wrote to the curator of the exhibition, Bruno Corà, that by showing those dark works I wished to announce the start of the White Year, with the aim of turning the idea of darkness into light. It was like seeing the glimmer of the end of the tunnel of those years of terrorism. As an oxymoron I presented several black volumes, entitling the exhibition *White Year*. The title had nothing to do with the pieces on display, but announced a project in which the entire year that was about to start would enter my work, like reality into a mirror. Thus a work with a dimension in time as well as in space. Over the course of 1989 I cast large surfaces of plaster and cut square slabs of white marble, to serve as the giant pages of a newspaper ready to gather the facts of the year. The rapid succession of events concluded at the beginning of November, with the collapse of the Berlin Wall and the consequent end of the Cold War. So that extraordinary development came at the conclusion of the *White Year*.

The Third Paradise, on the other hand, opens a course in time to which no end has been set. With *White Year* I signed the work, because it was clearly circumscribed as if it were a picture. With the Third Paradise I am no longer the only author. The responsibility for its authorship extends to every other person. In this way the Third Paradise becomes an immanent, as much as a contingent work. In history we find examples of good ideas that when structured into concrete practices end up becoming fossilized and distorting the original intention. They are ideas entrusted to the world. Those who proposed them never thought that the original idea, aimed at bringing about change, would be used to block the very process of transformation that had been set in motion: and in the name of its creator. Bearing this in mind, the Third Paradise has been unpegged from my name, proposing a dynamics of change and transformation in which everyone takes part personally under his or her own name.

Discussing with a friend of Jewish origin the fact that his people are still waiting for a messiah, I put forward the idea that we can no longer identify the messiah as a single person, but that we are all prophets and messiahs, commencing with the people who have a greater responsibility on the artistic, cultural and scientific plane, even if they belong to different faiths.

The Third Paradise does not want to prophesy a future imbued with metaphysical hopes, but a responsible transformation that concerns every area of human life and channels everyone's mental and practical energies into attaining a balance between nature and artifice, reason and emotion, individual and society, public and private, global and local.

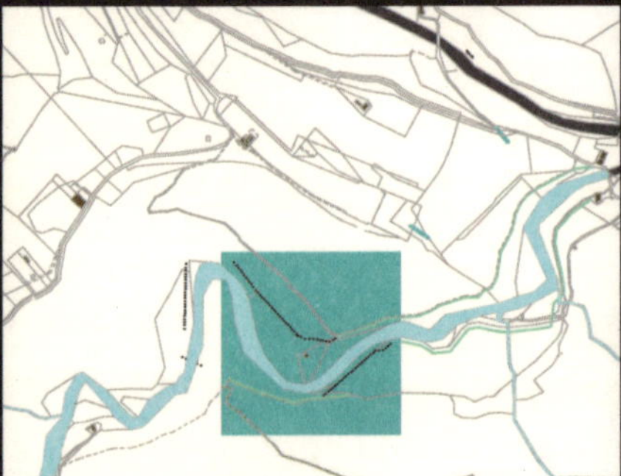

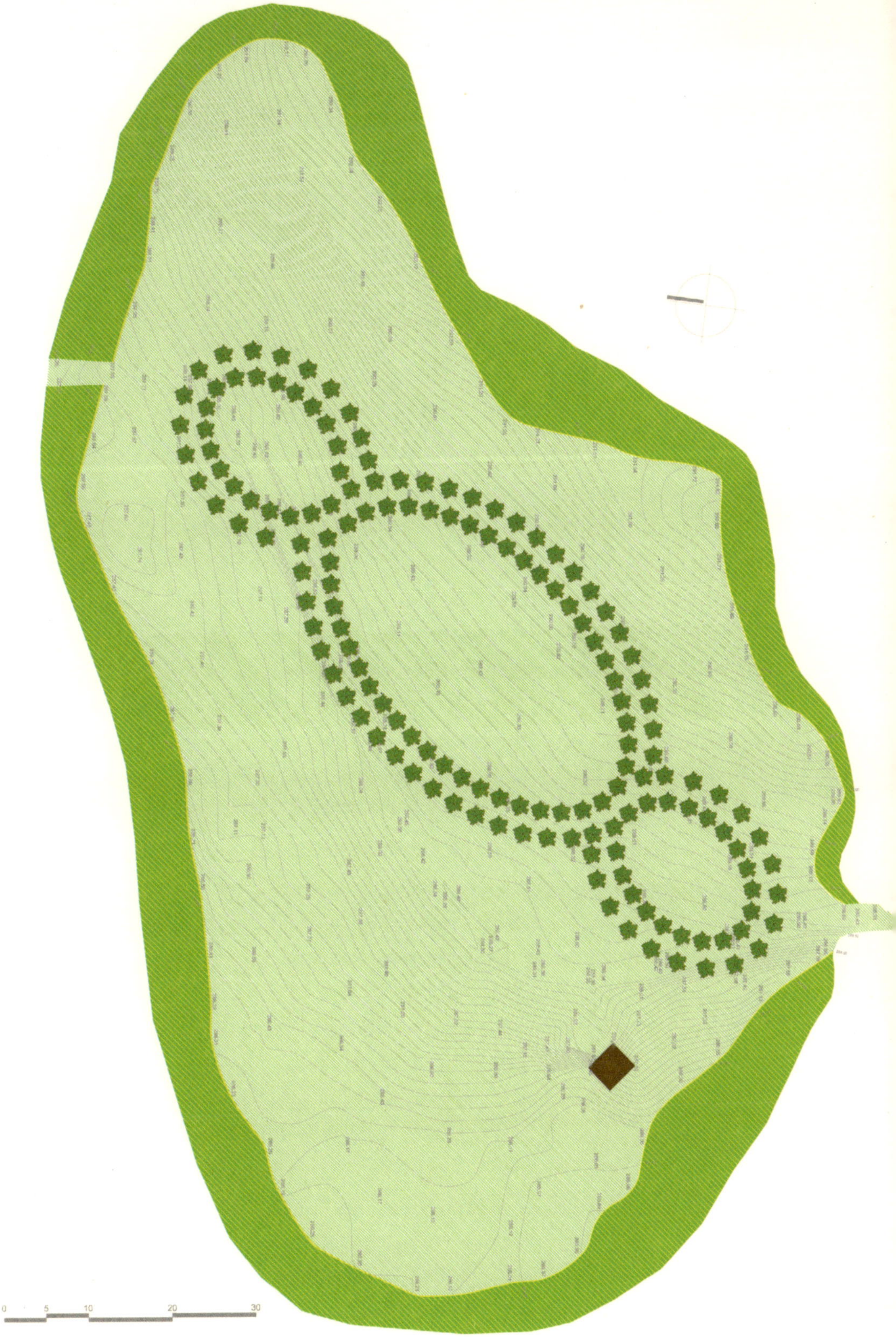
0
5
10
20
30

# Morality

We have reached the "moral of the story." It is said that every story has a moral, but it can also be said that every moral has a story. Morality is composed of myriads of stories, accounts, experiences and events that contain facts from which a useful lesson can be drawn for the processes to come. We can regard morality as the result of these experiences and the principle that generates new ones. In this sense morals become an essential part of the mechanism of life, as a pivot in every transition of human activity. Reality belies anyone who wishes to claim that morality is an independent, unique, absolute, static and immutable law. It can be inherited, but as with all legacies the credits and debts have to be assessed, so that the sound part can be reinvested in future projects. The Third Paradise unites the path in time followed by the two previous paradises and draws the moral that can serve us as a guide. Humanity feels the need for morality, sensing its crucial importance, but at the same time is conditioned, owing to the ways in which it is conventionally proposed, by a heaviness that weighs on thought, slowing and even paralyzing its fluidity. All this has created a mistrust in the very concept of morality in a growing number of people, who perceive it as a monolithic phenomenon to be accepted as an assumption and not as a verifiable result. So it is important to free humanity from this dead weight, by treating morality as a living and not a burdensome experience, and one in which we participate in a dynamic way.

As an artist I look at the past through the images that it hands down to me. Already as a boy I was spellbound by the full-page reproductions of Michelangelo's *Last Judgment* in the Sistine Chapel that I found in the Treccani encyclopedia my father kept in his library. That work attracted me in an almost obsessive fashion because of the sense of fateful tragedy that it conveyed. The images brought me face to face with an extreme and insurmountable limit. They heralded something so terrible that it would lead to the "end of the world." I understood neither why nor how that event, so powerfully described, could take place. I grew up and became a painter myself, and for some time I did not consider the possibility that I would find myself, personally, in the scene of that fresco. At a certain point, though, I began to realize that that catastrophic event might occur in my own lifetime. The means and causes by which such a prediction could come true began, in fact, to reveal themselves. Michelangelo found these prophecies inscribed in religious imagery: evidently in antiquity there was already a sense that beyond a certain level of growth that artificial world, fruit of the human "will," would not be able to go and would result in the end in total collapse. Today the reasons why such a collapse has become possible are explained in all the newspapers and shown to us daily on television screens all over the world.

*previous pages*
*Third Paradise Clearing,*
FAI (Fondo per l'Ambiente Italiano), Bosco di Francesco, Assisi (Perugia), 2010

It might be thought that the grounds for this apocalyptic vision, to use a term that we find in the scriptures, lie solely in technical questions, such as the warming of the planet due to greenhouse gases and other objective factors that have already been described here. I have tried to show how these are in fact directly related to the moral question. The greater the responsibility for the practical facts, the greater the moral significance of resolving or on the contrary irremediably aggravating the problem. So along with a reconsideration of the technical and practical aspects we have to look at the morality that has guided us to this point.

When I assert that today we all find ourselves in front of the mirror and become our own judges, what I am trying to say is that everyone assumes his own responsibility in a contract he has signed with society. At the same time, however, I think that society must redefine its collective morals by modifying all those terms that contain defects and vices which can no longer be tolerated. People are individually faced with themselves in the mirror, but all together they place humanity in front of judgment as a whole: that is why the last judgment is also referred to as the universal judgment in the Catholic faith. In the fresco in the Sistine Chapel the apocalypse does not end in nothing, but has a sequel: Heaven and Hell. For me the sequel is the Third Paradise, a heaven on Earth in which the reasons that have led to the infernal consequences which threatened to swallow up humanity today are absorbed and dissolved.

It is a problem that we have to sort out ourselves. There is no entity outside the cosmos that can dictate the new moral code–as was believed in the past–and nor can some individual arrogate this right to himself. We have seen too many examples of moral dictatorship and we bewail their devastating consequences. So we must take stock of the situation and see what humanity as a whole can offer itself, bearing in mind the scientific and cultural achievements that have been made. According to Darwinian theory we have moved from the elementary stages of cellular life to that of *Homo tecnologicus*. Today we find ourselves in an artificial world that is increasingly taking the place of the natural one and in it progress is not just for one part of the species, but for everyone. Science and technology, in fact, bring advances that can be shared by humanity as a whole. No longer are we dealing with passages of adaptation to natural environments, as in the past. Now the passage is determined by the possibility or impossibility of access to the advances made in the artificial environment. This condition is no longer linked to a capacity for adaptation intrinsic in the human species, but is a dependence on the artificial system that has been established and that can arbitrarily include or exclude part of humanity.

If the power exists, therefore, to bar access to the progress achieved, then to make use of such power is deplorable. The attainment of new abilities on the natural plane was morally acceptable, but the imposition of a state of inferiority is morally unacceptable. The injustice that some human beings deliberately do to other human beings is detrimental with respect to real progress, which now has to be for every individual: this is because all the kinds of harm that stem from progress itself affect the whole of humanity. So there is, in addition to the benefit that progress brings, also a responsibility for the harm that must be shared. The civilization in which we want to live is not exclusive to some while excluding others; scientific progress has given us the possibility of attaining a new level of humanity and thus giving meaning to the concept of "human," both as a noun and as an adjective. "The man who eats man" may be as powerful as a lion in the jungle, but he is backward in the human and moral sense, and keeps the humanity around him in a backward state. Even when utilizing the most advanced science it is possible, in fact, to be backward. It is indispensable to cultivate an economic micro-dynamics capable of providing all with the means to make use of advanced technology. The computer and the internet offer the possibility of sharing knowledge and understanding on a worldwide and individual level. Making computers at very low cost, within the reach of all the children on Earth, could be a moral act of economics, without lapsing into any kind of moralism. We must be careful, however, not to turn advanced technology into a faith to which we must always and indiscriminately adhere. Let us take all the possibilities of today's world, the positive and the negative, the functions and the dysfunctions of the modern system in its complexity, and try to make them converge in a domestic dimension of morality, in which the concept of predation does not dominate. A domestic sphere that comprises the home, the family, friends and the simplest relationships, embracing the best part of coexistence and the rapport between people. Even the animals that live in the home with us are able to overcome their instinct of predation. So both humanity and nature can be tamed–rising as far as possible above the concept of aggression for survival–and to succeed in this is for me a moral act. It is not so when human beings or animals are domesticated to use them as means in one's own system of predation.

Francesco Bernardone, the poor man of Assisi, had perhaps understood that this sense of domesticity could be extended to the world, starting with animals and including the whole of nature. Social custom, however, did not favor his ideals. Even the Church that made him a saint was an expression of those customs, to the point where in the same century it even used Francis's thought, through Franciscanism, to guide the persecutory arm of the Inquisition.

Today it is time for this custom to change. Speaking of religions, we also need to reconsider the laws that they have introduced in the absence of civil laws capable of dispensing justice impartially. Certainly they have had a decisive function on the social plane. Many problems of health, hygiene and the organization of community life have required strategies of a fideistic nature, which rely on the fear of God as the only possibility of making life work at the practical level. But if particular solutions may be regarded as indispensable at some moments in history, when the motives that have given rise to them change, they become outdated and turn into problems in their own right. Many of the laws that religions had seen as necessary solutions, despite no longer being valid, continue even today to keep people's minds dependent on devitalized systems. In this way precisely those who claim to be the dispensers of morality turn into vehicles of immorality.

It is up to us to find in our own sense of morality the response to the clearly recognizable necessities of today's world, such as survival, the protection of health, wellbeing in coexistence, free education for all, the right to knowledge and the social responsibility that ensues from all these pressing needs. Access to the Third Paradise requires a change of direction, one that has to be established by passing the educational methods of the past through the sieve of a new morality: methods shaped by rules, laws and even dogmas that still constitute the bases of schooling in our society.

During a performance in 1976, I wrote on a wall "Does God exist? Yes, here I am!" This declaration deconstructs the pyramidal structure at the top of which is set an absolute master, typical of monotheism. The voice of that entity comes from the mind and the mouth of the people who have helped to build that pyramid with their hands. The monotheistic religions have contributed to the hierarchical and political structuring of the various peoples, between which monstrous conflicts have then arisen.

"Yes, here I am!" signifies that everyone is god, and thus there is no longer just one god, as he is found in all people: the concept of monotheism has been replaced by that of omnitheism. If my daughter or my nephew were to ask me "Does God exist?," I would answer "Yes, you are God!" Every person, even from the biological point of view, is a Third Paradise in so far as he or she is the union of two signs, female and male, just as nature and artifice are united in the symbol. From this combination each person is born different from the next. It follows that the democratic morality of the Third Paradise is love and respect for differences. If the biological function of the parents is understood, then it also becomes possible to understand the politics that can bring about a balanced domestic administration of the whole of society from a meeting of opposites.

The great painting of the *Last Judgment* had been commissioned from Michelangelo by the Church of Rome and represented Christ in the act of judging humanity, some time in the future. My fresco is the mirror, commissioned directly by the artist, which places humanity in front of itself for "judgment" in the present time. So in this work there is an assumption of responsibility both on the part of the artist and on the part of every single person who directly, indirectly or even ideally is faced with his or her own image.

It is up to each of them to interpret, on the basis of his or her own "judgment," the moral of this story.

# Biography

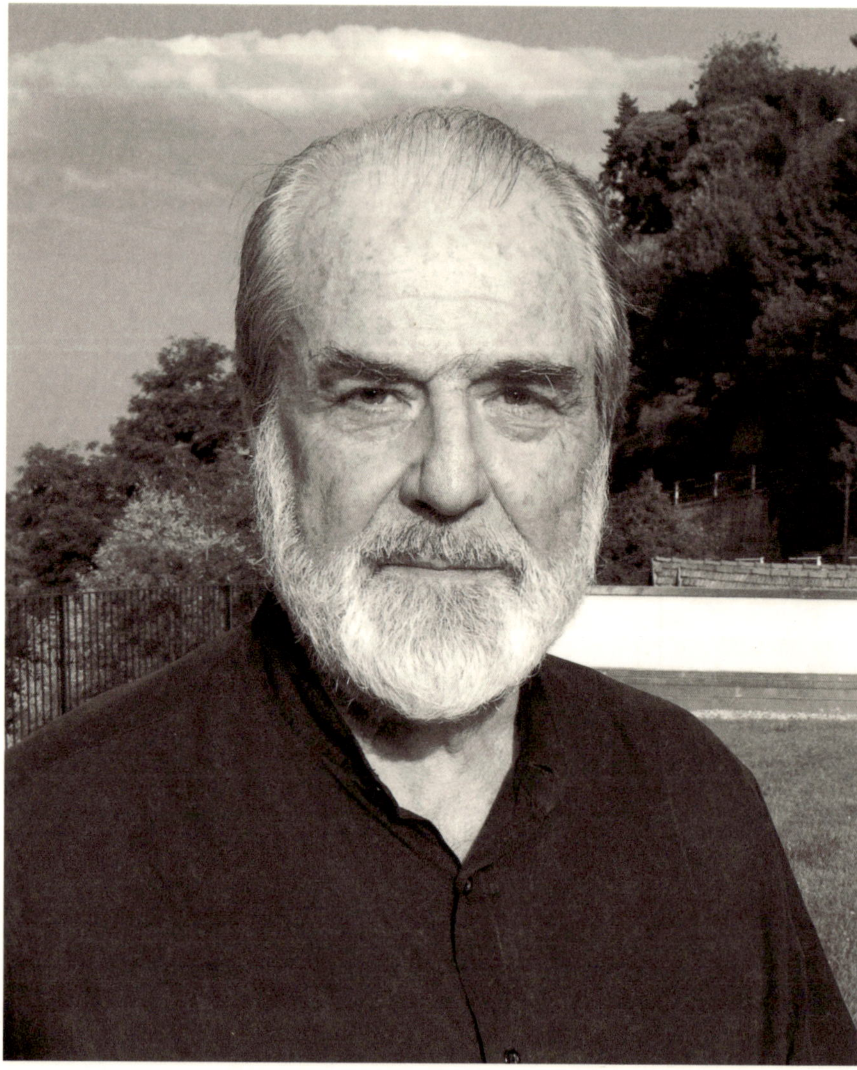

# Michelangelo Pistoletto

Born in Biella in 1933. His artistic training began in the studio of his father, a painter and restorer, where he went to work at the age of fourteen. He subsequently attended Armando Testa's advertising design school.

In 1955 he began to exhibit the results of the inquiry into self-portraiture that characterized his painting in the late fifties. He received the San Fedele Prize in Milan in 1958. In 1960 he had his first solo show at Galleria Galatea in Turin. That same year he made several life-sized self-portraits on gold, silver and copper monochrome backgrounds. In 1961 he created the series of works entitled *The Present*, painting his own image on a black background to which a layer of transparent varnish gave a mirror gloss.

In 1962 he perfected the technique of his *Mirror Paintings*: he produced an image on tissue paper by enlarging a photograph to life size, painting it with the tip of a brush, then affixed it onto a sheet of mirror-finished stainless steel (after 1971 the painted tissue was replaced by a silkscreen of the photographic image). These works directly include the viewer and real time, and open up perspective, reversing the Renaissance perspective that had been closed by the twentieth-century avant-gardes. *The Mirror Paintings*, shown for the first time in March 1963 at Galleria Galatea, quickly brought Pistoletto international acclaim and led to his inclusion in major exhibitions of Pop Art and Nouveau Realisme. During the sixties the artist had solo shows in important galleries and museums in Europe and the United States (in 1964 at Galerie Sonnabend in Paris, in 1966 at the Walker Art Center in Minneapolis, in 1967 at the Palais des Beaux Arts in Brussels, in 1969 at the Boijmans van Beuningen Museum in Rotterdam). In 1967 he received the Belgian critics' prize and that of the São Paulo Biennale. *The Mirror Paintings* are the foundation of Pistoletto's subsequent artistic output and of the theoretical thought that consistently parallels it.

In 1964, at Galleria Sperone in Turin, he showed the body of work called *Plexiglass*—a first transposition in real space of the new open dimension of the mirror paintings, as well as a declaration of art's "conceptual" character.

In 1965-1966 he showed a set of works, entitled *Minus Objects*, in his studio. These works, made in the contingent dimension of time and based on the principle of difference, broke with the dogma of the uniformity of individual artistic style. They are considered

fundamental to the birth of Arte Povera, an art movement theorized by Germano Celant in 1967, of which Pistoletto was a an animating force and a leading figure.
In March, 1967 Pistoletto began to work outside traditional exhibition spaces. In December of that year he announced the opening of his studio, in a manifesto. In this context The Zoo arose—a group of people from different artistic disciplines, together with whom Pistoletto carried out actions conceived as creative collaborations from 1968 to 1970. Invited to the Venice Biennale in 1968, he published his *Manifesto of Collaboration.*
Between October 1975 and September 1976 Pistoletto carried out a work that was intended to fill a full year. Divided into twelve consecutive exhibitions, entitled *The Rooms*, the piece occupied the spaces of Galleria Stein in Turin. It was the first of a series of complex works, each developed over a year's time and named "time continents". Other works from the series are *White Year* (1989) and *Happy Turtle* (1992). In 1976 he published *One Hundred Exhibitions in the Month of October*, a booklet that describes a hundred ideas for works conceived over a month, many of which he carried out in the following years.
In March 1978, in a show at Galleria Persano in Turin, Pistoletto defined two main directions his future artwork would take: *Division and Multiplication of the Mirror* and *Art Takes On Religion.* In this same month he began a one-year residency at DAAD in Berlin, in which city he presented a retrospective exhibition at the Nationalgalerie and in thirteen public places.
Over the two-year period, 1978-1979, he presented a series of one-person shows, installations and actions in cities across the United States. This included *Creative Collaboration* in Atlanta, a broad creative partnership extended to the entire city, in which he involved local artists from different disciplines together with artists with whom he had worked in the past (actor Lionello Gennero, musician Enrico Rava, composer Morton Feldmann) and members of his family. His artistic collaborations continued throughout 1979 in different places, particularly at Corniglia (Liguria), a village with whose inhabitants he staged the play Anno Uno at the Teatro Qurino in Rome in 1981.
In 1981, at Salvatore Ala Gallery in New York, Pistoletto showed *The Nativity*, a first example of the rigid polyurethane sculptures he created in the early eighties. In 1984 he remade some of these works in marble and on a large scale in his one-person show at Forte di Belvedere in Florence.
From 1985 to 1989 he created a new cycle of works, made up of surfaces and volumes in anonymous materials and dark, gloomy colors, called *Art of Squalor.*
In 1991 he was appointed Professor of Sculpture at the Vienna Fine Arts Academy, a position he kept until 1999. With his students, he developed an innovative program intent on breaking down the traditional barriers between artistic disciplines.
In 1993 he began the phase called *Art Sign*, based on an idea conceived in *One Hundred Exhibitions in the Month of October* (1976). In addition to producing a series of works sharing a form that constituted his personal *Art Sign*, the artist invited other people, on diverse occasions, to create and present an *Art Sign* of their own.
In 1994 began *Project Art* with which Pistoletto—by means of a program manifesto, public meetings, displays and exhibitions that involved artists of different disciplines and representatives of broad sectors of society—placed art at the center of socially responsible change.
1998 witnessed the establishment of *Cittadellarte-Fondazione Pistoletto* in a former mill

in Biella, Italy, acquired by the artist in 1991. Here the goals expressed in *Project Art* are still being developed and accomplished.

2000 saw the inauguration, at the Paoli-Calmettes Cancer Institute in Marseille, of the *Place of Meditation and Prayer*, a multiconfessional, secular space conceived and executed by the artist.

In 2002 Pistoletto was Artistic Director of the Turin International Biennial of Young Art entitled *Big Social Game*. That same year he received the Diploma di Benemerito della Cultura e dell'Arte from the President of the Italian Republic.

In 2003 he was awarded the Golden Lion for Lifetime Achievement at the Venice Biennale. At the same Biennale he presented *Love Difference - Artistic Movement for an Inter-Mediterranean Politic*, a project born in April 2002 at Cittadellarte, for which Pistoletto made a large reflecting table in the shape of the Mediterranean basin, around which many of the subsequent activities of *Love Difference* took place.

In 2004 Turin University graduated him with a laurea honoris causa in Political Science. On that occasion the artist publicly announced the most recent phase of his work, *Third Paradise*, the symbol of which is the *New Infinity Sign* he created in 2003.

In 2007, in Jerusalem, Pistoletto was awarded the Wolf Foundation Prize in the Arts, "for his constantly inventive career as an artist, educator and activist whose restless intelligence has created prescient forms of art that contribute to fresh understanding of the world."

*His works are present in the collections of leading museums of modern and contemporary art, including:* MOMA, New York; Guggenheim Museum, New York; Beaubourg, Paris; Galleria Nazionale d'Arte Moderna, Rome; Museo d'Arte Contemporanea, Seul; Municipal Museum of Art, Toyota; Museo Reina Sophia, Madrid; MACBA, Barcellona; Hirshhorn Museum and Sculpture Garden, Washington; Museo d'Arte Contemporanea, Rivoli; Tate Modern, London.

He has participated eleven times in the Venice Biennale (1966, 1968, 1976, 1978, 1984, 1986, 1993, 1995, 2003, 2005, 2009) and four times in Documenta, Kassel (1968, 1982, 1992 and 1997).

*Principal one-person museum shows:*

1966, Walker Art Center, Minneapolis; 1967, Palais des Beaux Arts, Brussels; 1969, Boymans van Beuningen Museum, Rotterdam; 1973, Kestner Gesellschaft, Hannover; 1974, Matildenhohe, Darmstadt; 1976, Palazzo Grassi, Venezia; 1978, Nationalgalerie, Berlin; 1979, Rice Demenil Museum, Houston; 1983, Palacio de Cristal, Madrid; 1984, Forte di Belvedere, Firenze; 1988, P.S.1, New York; Staatliche Kunsthalle, Baden Baden; 1989, Kunsthalle, Bern; Secession, Vienna; 1990, Galleria Nazionale d'Arte Moderna, Rome; 1991, Museet for Samditkunst, Oslo; 1993, Deichtorhallen, Hamburg; 1994, National Museum of Contemporary Art, Seoul; 1995, Museum des 20. Jahrhunderts, Wien; 1996, Lenbachhaus, Munich; 1997, Centro per l'Arte Contemporanea Luigi Pecci, Prato; 1999, MMAO, Oxford; Henry Moore Foundation, Halifax; Galerie Taxispalais, Innsbruck; 2000: GAM, Turin; MACBA, Barcelona; Fondazione Burri, Città di Castello; 2001, Contemporary Museum of Bosnia, Sarajevo; Ludwig Museum, Budapest; 2003, MuHKA, Antwerp; 2005, Galleria Civica, Modena; 2007, MAMAC, Nice.

*Printed by*
Grafiche Antiga, Crocetta del Montello (Treviso)
for Marsilio Editori© s.p.a in Venice



FSC
**Mixed Sources**
Product group from well-managed forests and other controlled sources
www.fsc.org Cert no. SA-COC-002023
© 1996 Forest Stewardship Council



edition
10 9 8 7 6 5 4 3 2 1

year
2010 2011 2012 2013 2014 2015